WHERE HAVE I BEEN ALL MY LIFE?

How I Finally Grew Up After a Life of
Putting Up, Giving Up and Shutting Up

LISA BENSON

Where Have I Been All My Life?:
How I Finally Grew Up After a Life of Putting Up, Giving Up and Shutting Up

lisabensonauthor.com

Copyright © 2022 Lisa Benson

Second edition published in Australia 2025
Published by Lisa Benson

All rights reserved. No part of this book may be used or reproduced by any means, graphic, electronic, or mechanical, including photocopying, recording, taping or by any information storage retrieval system without the written permission of the author except in the case of brief quotations embodied in critical articles and reviews. Likewise, no portion of this book may be posted to a website or distributed by any other means without securing the advanced written permission of the author.

Because of the dynamic nature of the Internet, any web addresses or links contained in this book may have changed since publication and may no longer be vaild. The views expressed in this work are solely those of the author.

The author of this book does not dispense medical advice or prescribe or advocate the use of any techniques as a form of treatment for physical, mental, emotional, or medical problems. Every case is different and the advice of a physician should be sought before taking action. The intent of the author is only to offer information of a general nature as it relates to her own real-world experience. In the event you use any of the information in this book for yourself, the author assumes no responsibility for your actions.

National Library of Australia Catalogue-in-Publication data:
Where Have I Been All My Life?/Lisa Benson

ISBN: 978-1-7638604-0-7 (hb)
ISBN: 978-1-7638604-1-4 (sc)
ISBN: 978-1-7638604-2-1 (e)

Printed in Australia, the USA, Canada and Europe.

For Mum.
I am me, because of you.

CONTENTS

Preface ix
Introduction xi

PART ONE: Putting Up 1

1. G-String Pyjamas 3
2. Believing Myths 12
3. Cheating Boyfriend 21
4. Cheating Self 29
5. Warped Values 40
6. Mothering Man-Boys 48
7. Stolen Grief 55
8. Guilty When Innocent 63
9. Wasted Time 71
10. Puzzling Allergies 76

PART TWO: Giving Up 85

11. Spiritual Recipe 87
12. Relinquishing Blame 95
13. Saying Yes 103

14. Happy Families 109
15. Welcoming Intruders..115
16. Spunky Spirit 120
17. Taking Risks 127
18. Childless Woman 132
19. My Old Life 141

PART THREE: Shutting Up 149
20. Unexpected Visitors 151
21. Secret Desires 156
22. Future Fears 162
23. Finding My Voice..167
24. Unpacking My Childhood 175

PART FOUR: Growing Up 185
25. Taking Responsibility..187
26. Life Happens for Me 194
27. No Getting Better 202
28. The Family Tree..210
29. Reframing Firsts..220
30. Letting Go 227
31. A Place for All 233
32. Seeing Clearly...240
33. Choosing My Name 249
34. Trusting My Future 253

Conclusion: Let Me Fly...259
Acknowledgements...270
About the Author...275

PREFACE

Memoir is one person's view of a particular time in their life from their unique perspective. I have done my utmost to recollect all events as accurately as possible. When I have not expressly asked permission, I have used fictional names and changed specific details in an effort to keep the identities private of those who have not chosen to be part of my story.

I have no intention to cause harm or defame anyone and have included only what is required to maintain the emotional truth of my story. Where appropriate, I have concentrated emotions and feelings to a particular group of people, so I am not singling out an individual person.

When making editing decisions, I took time to consider each incident carefully and passed every scene through three gates: Is it true? Is it kind? Is it necessary? Everything I've written in this book is a true account of the events and emotions as I have experienced them. Nothing is made up. I endeavoured to be kind at all times, and the pieces that remain are the ones I feel are necessary to tell this story while taking my readers on an emotional journey.

My book should not be considered as advice – it is a story, my story. My hope is that you feel its resonance, and after reading it, may you feel less alone.

INTRODUCTION

My story isn't about an extraordinary life. It's quite the opposite. My ordinary life is a cautionary tale. A warning. An example of what not to do. I wrote it for those of you who have ever felt stuck or lost hope for the future.

During my twenties and thirties – in the prime of my life – I spent fifteen years in bad relationships. Why? Because I was a perfectionist. I know this sounds like a contradiction (Why would a perfectionist put up with unfulfilling relationships?). But hang in there with me. There were other reasons. I'll get to those.

Before I could move on, I had to understand why I'd made such terrible choices with far-reaching consequences. The truth is, I didn't actually grow up until I was in my forties (yet another contradiction). Through my childhood and teens, I'd always been the mature one, the goody-goody, the textbook example to follow.

None of it made any sense. I only understand it now as I look back.

For decades, I had unknowingly pushed the pause button on my life, tumble-weeding through time, frozen by anxiety and hiding from my fears. I was waiting for everything to fall into place before I pressed play and went after my goals.

That's when my real life will begin, I kept telling myself. I had pushed 'living' to the side in a pile of things to do, as if it were merely a tax return that hadn't been lodged. If I hadn't been struck by a wake-up call to shake me out of my madness, I may have waited forever.

If I had my time over, I would prefer not to have made so many costly sacrifices. It's impossible to go back and change the past, but once we know better, we can live the rest of our days differently.

I want to share my mistakes with you in the hope that you do not fritter away precious time figuring out this stuff, like I did.

As I approached forty, I hadn't really been in love, let alone been married, and I knew I'd almost certainly missed out on the opportunity to have children. My reality was so far removed from where I'd wished it as a little girl.

You were supposed to have it sorted by now, I'd often reprimand myself.

I had put up with partners who didn't value me, stayed too long in dead-end relationships and deadening jobs, and held back speaking my truth for all the wrong reasons.

But it wasn't too late. It never is.

This book is the map of how I worked through my suffering

Praise for *Where Have I Been All My Life?*

'*Where Have I Been All My Life?* is a tribute to one woman's search to find her voice and freedom after a lifetime of being told who she should be. Lisa's journey through self-doubt and invisibility will resonate with every woman who has ever recoiled from owning her own power and choices for fear of making mistakes and disappointing others. As she explores the intergenerational forces that shaped her, she begins to outgrow their strictures and finally make decisions that bring her home to her truest self. This is a love story for every woman who needs to learn to honour and respect herself.'

JOANNE FEDLER - INTERNATIONAL BESTSELLING AUTHOR

'The book starts with a heart-felt intention for us to resonate with the story and "feel less alone," and it delivers it beautifully. This is a journey of how someone reclaims her self, her beauty, her purpose, and her being. It's inspirational and motivational. I rooted for Lisa as she took us through her journey, and now I want to do the same for myself, and shed those final bits of me that have been holding me back. Lisa expertly draws from different moments of her life to illustrate the lessons she has learned along the way. She starts with what already seems like a big "issue," and slowly peels the layers to show us deeper "issues" and thus deeper insights. It's clear, from this memoir, that we are a result of the accumulation of our experiences. Lisa shares how she accumulated these nuggets of wisdom, and how she learned to trust herself, her inner guidance, and reclaim her life. In sharing her story, she shares a deep perspective that can help transform your life.'

SONEE SINGH - AUTHOR AND POET

'*Where Have I Been All My Life?* is more than one woman's story. It's a guidebook to hand down to your daughter, give to a friend or keep for your own source of truth and empowerment. After reading the book, my idea for the cover came after having an epiphany. My vision was of a 1970/80's ballerina musical box symbolising perfection, with the rose petals representing growth and the shedding of expectations. The mountains illustrate life's obstacles along the journey. I used a mix of structured and playful fonts and colours to appeal to a wide female audience. It was also important to specifically represent the personality of the author and how far she has come. I know this book will be a source of light for so many.'

**LAUREN HARPER (HARPER BRANDING & DESIGN)
- COVER DESIGNER**

and turned roadblocks into doorways to growth.

Realising I was stuck was just the start of my transition. I had to reverse my conditioning, one step at a time, to grasp and fully understand the reasons I'd settled for unhappiness. As each layer peeled away, I became more open and expansive. My awakening was like buying bonus years. I just had to go where I'd never been before – deep inside my heart.

I had spent my life fulfilling other peoples' expectations of me, rather than figuring out what I wanted to do. I played small and suppressed my inner nature, limited by the beliefs, fears and expectations of others.

As it turns out, I began writing the book that I needed to read. I had always expected the answers to Life's Big Questions to miraculously appear:

What is the meaning of my life?
Who am I?
What am I here for?
Why am I like this?
How did I get here?

I began writing well before I had any of the answers and have been plagued by procrastination and self-sabotage throughout the process. I have been paralysed by fears of not being good enough and worries about what others would think, traits that have followed me throughout my life. Let me tell you, perfectionism wears you down. I've been constantly *trying* instead of *being*, procrastinating instead of doing. I've been waiting for permission and my dreams to magically come true.

Stronger forces are at play though, and now here I am, speaking up for the first time in my life. In doing so, I've discovered how much of my suffering has been entangled in other peoples'.

Once I dealt with compounded loss and grief in my late thirties, I realised I had a story worth telling – three stories, actually: the one I'd told the world, the one I'd told myself, and the real one – the truth. That's the one I'm sharing with you here. If my vulnerability can shine some light into your life, that will have made this entire painful experience worthwhile.

I see and hear of so many others who are in similar circumstances, wasting time, waiting for the right time to make changes or hanging in just a little longer. It pains me to see them putting up with mistreatment and manipulation in the process.

I have squeezed more into the last ten years of my life than in the preceding thirty-seven, and I couldn't be more excited to share my story with you.

It's taken me a while, but I'm ready now.

Sometimes we have to go back, way back, before we have the courage to move forward.

PART ONE
Putting Up

1

G-STRING PYJAMAS

I felt the rush of warm air on the back of my neck. Over the past three years, Adrian had become an expert in creeping up on me.

'What does *twice in one week* mean?'

He'd heard the crickets chirping from the other side of the room as a text message arrived on my phone. He'd been watching TV as I unpacked the groceries and had gotten up and come to stand over my shoulder. His reaction was a response to the private text my friend Michelle had sent me, which he felt was his right to read. I closed my eyes, put my hand on my stomach and sucked in a big breath before I turned around. I could hear my heartbeat in my ears.

I didn't have time to think of an excuse. I just blurted out the truth.

'A guy just asked me out while I was at the shops – that's all.'

'What?' He was silent for a couple of seconds. 'That'd be right.' The vein on his temple was throbbing. 'Who is he?'

'I've got *no* idea.'

I picked the cold groceries off the bench and brushed past Adrian to the fridge.

'Well, why would you tell Michelle then? Huh? What would you do that for? I can't believe you would tell *her*. You must know who he is.'

Adrian was getting louder. And closer. His forehead, the tip of his finger, they were not far from my face.

'She was at the shops at the same time as me and she forgot her card, so I paid for her groceries. She's going to pay me back tomorrow.'

'How could you do this? So what did he say to you? Far out.'

Adrian had a look on his face I hadn't seen before. He'd never hit me. Not yet. But his eyes hated me. My heart was *ka-thunk, ka-thunk, ka-thunk*ing.

'Can't you see it was nothing?' I tried to calm my breath so I could get the words out right. 'I was in the fruit and veggie section, and a guy came over and said, "I don't want to step on anyone's toes, but I just saw you there and was wondering if you would like to go and have a coffee sometime." And I said, "Thank you, that's lovely of you but I actually have a partner," and he went away. That's *it*. Nothing else. I didn't do *anything* wrong. You're making it out as if it's my fault. I can't help what other people say or do.'

I didn't dare tell him that I had found it flattering.

'Why didn't you tell me then? And why did you tell Michelle?'

'Because I knew this is exactly how you'd react.' I picked up a tea towel and slapped it against the bench. Hard. 'And I told you, Michelle was there. I'll ring her so she can tell you herself.'

'And what did she mean by *twice*?'

Argh.

I called Michelle. I had become used to this kind of interrogation. But I was tired of it.

'Another guy just gave me a compliment the other day in the stre—Hi, Shell. Adrian just read your text message and I wanted you to tell him what happened at the shops because he doesn't believe me.'

I heard a faint 'Oh no.'

'Talk to Michelle. She'll tell you that nothing happened. Why don't you just believe me?'

'I don't want to speak to her.' His voice thundered.

I quickly ended the call, though poor Michelle would have been worried. But something in me burst from the stress, and I began to cry. Not the tears-rolling-down-the-face sort of crying. It was ugly, animated, noisy. I couldn't help it. I hated who I had become.

I'm such an idiot. How did this happen? Can the neighbours hear these ridiculous arguments? They must think I'm crazy for putting up with this.

At times, it felt like I was in a straitjacket with no-one to untie me.

When I daydreamed as a child, I used to imagine a bubble form of transportation, like the aero cars in *The Jetsons* cartoon, only more graceful. In that moment with Adrian, I wanted that pink fairy bubble of my childhood fantasy to transport me to another place. Anywhere. But instead, at thirty-four, Little Miss Perfect was stuck in a far-from-perfect relationship, putting up with a far-from-perfect job. I must have contracted Stockholm syndrome somewhere along the way.

As I stood there, shaking with tears, I wondered what Shaun in music class at high school would have to say. I could picture his face. I could hear his voice.

'Oh, miss, please, can I just get *one* more mark?' He'd stood up, pointing his index finger at me. 'I just want to beat Miss Perfect at something. She even beat the boys in woodwork and metalwork. It's not fair. She comes first in everything.'

If only he could see me now. Miss Goody-Two-Shoes-Straighty-One-Eighty, who cried when she got a B, had received a big fat F in relationships. How could a woman who appeared to get everything right in her life get the most important decisions so wrong?

At school, we were taught about the different types of clouds, the planets in the solar system and how to dissect a rat; but the curriculum didn't teach me how to choose the right partner. My parents didn't teach me that either. They had been together since their teenage years, just like both sets of my grandparents.

If I can bear to admit it, this wasn't my first time. A one-off mistake could be forgiven. This was the *third* time I had ended up in a relationship with the wrong person.

My older sister, Kim, had done the same in her early twenties. She ended up marrying a man she knew wasn't right for her. She should have cancelled the wedding but hadn't wanted to disappoint anyone. The marriage didn't last even two years, but the horrible memories stayed.

I clearly remember Mum once saying to me, 'Whatever you do, stay boring.'

We had been talking about Kim's relationship dramas. I was several years into my first humdrum relationship. Almost ten years later, I was nowhere closer to where I wanted to be. Here I was, being interrogated by an insecure man about an innocuous comment made to me in passing by a possibly less insecure man.

Eventually, after he'd expended all his rage that night, Adrian left me alone. While he brooded, I went back to my domestic duties. I cooked the tuna bake I'd made so many times I didn't even have to think. I was used to surviving on autopilot. My weekly schedule was rigid and repetitive. And herein was the problem: in my life, I was doing the same things so many times that I had become robotic.

I desperately wanted to crawl into bed, but I didn't want to be anywhere near Adrian who'd had a bubble bath and had gone to sleep without saying goodnight. Instead, I stared blankly at the TV, not caring what was on.

When I eventually snuck into bed I slipped into the sheets in my G-string. Somehow that night, this habit jarred in a way it hadn't before.

For the first few months of our relationship, Adrian kept a photo in his wallet of his ex-girlfriend flashing her G-stringed butt at the camera, as if she were waiting to receive it doggy style.

'What's that still doing in there?' I asked.

'Oh, that's Bianca. You need to give me a photo like this to replace it.' He laughed. He found G-strings sexy. So I wore mine to bed every night.

Who puts up with that sort of shit? Me, clearly. Because there I was. Those G-strings were so damn uncomfortable, but I still continued to put them on before I got into bed.

I fell into a fitful sleep that night, wondering as I so often seemed to do, *What the hell is wrong with me?*

'Are you okay?' Rachael asked as I walked into the office the next morning. I'd been working with her for seven years and she'd become like a second mum to me. I didn't have the energy to explain my puffy bleak eyes.

'Yep, all good.'

If I mentioned the previous night, the tears would start flowing uncontrollably again.

I became used to pretending.

My workmates never questioned my frequently bloodshot eyes. I'd keep busy on the computer to avoid eye contact. My trusty lavender eye pillow was always ready in the fridge. Taking it to bed was as familiar as cleaning my teeth, washing my face and sleeping in those ridiculous G-strings. But people at work were polite. And I was dishonest, playing as if everything was *just fine*.

Why did I remain silent? I wanted to speak up, but I was unsure how to articulate my unhappiness. I knew I had dishonoured myself by accepting mistreatment from Adrian. It was impossible to explain and embarrassing to admit. *No-one would understand,* I thought. By pretending everything was okay, I was protecting myself from admitting my reality as well as taking action. I had no idea this meant I was enabling Adrian's behaviour. I was caught up in a shameful loop. The more time that passed, the more embedded I became in maintaining the facade.

This wasn't the first time I'd kept silent.

All my life, I'd tolerated bad behaviour from men. I'm lucky I escaped any single horrific incident, but there have been countless events I dismissed as 'nothing much.' They go back as far as my earliest memories. Even as a toddler, I used to think, 'Men look at me funny.' The toilets at preschool had glass walls. Whenever I needed to pee, I would cross my legs until the male teacher was out of sight.

When I was seven, I overheard a conversation at a tennis barbecue.

'I'd like to look under there,' a man with a moustache said as he angled his head towards me. He played tennis with my dad. My face turned warm. I tilted my head forward, pulling down on my frilly blue and purple skirt. He sniggered with his mate then sucked the froth off his can of Foster's beer.

During my commuting days I had an encounter with the serial train sleaze. He thigh wrestled me, pressing everything from his shoulder to his knee against my body. Adrenaline morphed my flesh into concrete. My 'fuck you' voice mustn't have been working that day.

The worst incident was with the father of one of my ex-boyfriends who cornered me in his office and roared with laughter as he dropped his pants to his ankles and exposed his genitals to me. I'd recently broken up with his son. Did that make me fair game? All I heard was the muffled *tick…tick… tick* of the wall clock. Everything slowed down and became blurry. I grabbed the knot on my scarf and tugged it free of my clammy neck.

'Ah…er…' He fumbled with his words as well as his zipper. I seized the opportunity and slithered through the gap between him and the door.

Right here, I'm confessing everything I've never said out loud. I was afraid if I did, people would look at me differently. Every time some man crossed the line, all I wanted was to move on and forget.

If I ignored these things, they never happened, right?

* * *

The following Wednesday night, Adrian was waiting for me when I arrived at the supermarket. He was usually at the gym then, where he spent most of his free time. But he wasn't there to help me shop. He didn't offer to push the trolley.

'Is he here?' he asked, scanning for an innocent man who had dared to compliment me.

I ignored him. But inside, I was boiling. Around me, casual shoppers seemed to be in functional relationships. The bright, fluorescent lights almost seemed to shine a spotlight on how wrong I had got this.

Were some of those other happy shoppers also just pretending everything was fine?

Adrian folded his hands over his stomach, like a bodyguard ready to pounce on anyone who came within a metre of me.

I knew I was being manipulated but never realised the extent of the unacceptable behaviour I was tolerating. I kept downplaying it until I convinced myself it wasn't *that* bad. I was confused because while he chipped away at my confidence,

Adrian also 'adored' me. I put his behaviour down to a lack of maturity. I assumed I could 'fix' him if I had enough time to counsel him.

Back in 2008, there wasn't a name for what I was experiencing. I would have never called it abuse. I wasn't aware emotional abuse or coercive control was a thing, let alone how serious or widespread it is. 'Coercive control' only became a recognised term many years later, and England was the first country that outlawed it in 2015. Coercive control is still dealt with under civil law in Australia, although it was proposed to be criminalised in a bill in October 2020.

I felt trapped in a predicament that had no name, no answers and without anyone to help me.

As Adrian continued to search for the offender and I filled the trolley with our weekly groceries, I knew one thing was certain: I *had* to get out even if it meant admitting I'd failed. Again.

Looking back now, I wish I'd realised sooner that leaving a destructive relationship and never wearing a bloody G-string to bed is the opposite of a failure.

2

BELIEVING MYTHS

'What's that?' I asked Dad as I pointed to what was hanging between his legs in the shower.

'That's my goddle.'

'Ah.'

Nanna had told me to wash my goddle whenever I stayed the night at her house, but I was pretty sure I didn't have one of those. I swung my head between my open legs to take a look. *Nope, definitely no goddle there.*

I was only four, but that was the last shower I ever took with Dad. I never heard Mum or Dad ever say *penis* or *vagina*. I assumed they were naughty words, off limits for Kim and me. *Goddle* was a word that Dad's side of the family used for anything related to those embarrassing bits. Mum preferred the term 'front bottom.'

A few years later a group of us were joking about other names for our rude bits after a sex education lesson at school.

'Doodle,' said Neal.

'Dinger donger,' said Belinda.

Our cheekbones felt bruised from laughing so hard.

'Goddle,' I said with confidence.

The laughter stopped.

'Huh? There's no such thing as a goddle,' Neal said.

'There is too. My dad said so.'

Neal began to laugh again and pointed at me.

I felt my face go hot. *Why would they lie to me? Why would they make up a stupid word? Did they think I was a baby?* I assumed everyone called it that.

Dad also told me that when there is a ring around the moon or the cows sit down in the paddock, it's a sign of rain.

'But why would they sit on the grass?' I questioned Dad.

'They're keeping it covered so they have dry food when the rain passes.'

I have since learnt that both of these are old wives' tales, but I still anticipate rain whenever I see a circle surrounding the moon or a cow resting in a grassy field. I've often wondered why it would matter if the grass got wet anyway.

Myths from my childhood followed me into adulthood and shaped my thoughts and behaviours.

When I was six, Mum and I visited my Nanna during the school holidays. Pop was at work at the Commonwealth Scientific and Industrial Research Organisation (CSIRO). When he wasn't working, he was doing crosswords, puzzles or eating lollies from the huge plastic jar that looked like a lantern with a yellow lid and handle.

Nanna put the kettle on.

'What are you going to be when you grow up, Lisa?' she asked.

I spun around with my hands gracefully above my head, 'I'm going to be a ball-e-rina.'

'Yeah, right. They are *all* precocious little brats,' Mum called out from the sunroom.

My smiley face disappeared faster than my spins.

'Well, maybe I'll be an actress, or a singer, or…a newsreader then?'

'You are certainly an actress, that's for sure.' Mum rolled her eyes at me as she entered the room. 'Kim is the arty one and Lisa is the smart one, so she'll probably be a lawyer, or a teacher, or something like that.'

Everything dropped – my head, shoulders, heels and imaginary tutu.

Expressionless, I looked up at Nanna. 'I'm going to be a teacher,' I whispered in her ear.

After that, I took dancing off my after-school activity list and played tennis instead.

Mum and Dad were both players – in fact, they met because of their love of the game. For most of my adolescence, Mum worked at Medicare, and Dad was a building supervisor. Before that, he was a builder and did roofing, guttering and cladding. Dad's after-work job was as a tennis coach, which meant I had a racquet in my hand from the age of four and started playing competitively at a young age. I craved my parents' approval, so

I didn't question why Mum didn't want me to dance. We never spoke of my dreams again.

And so my path in life began to be determined by others – parents, teachers, family, friends, the media and social pressures. Never me.

As a little girl, I had huge ambitions. I knew I was intelligent and capable. In Year One, my friend Cassandra and I were sent to the principal's office once a week to do extra schoolwork to keep our minds stimulated. We also helped teach the kindy kids how to read. Unlike Mum and Dad, who were content with working in safe jobs and paying off the mortgage, I wanted to explore the extremes of my potential. And I was born with the confidence to do it.

I recall strutting into my huge kindy classroom. Looking up at Ms Bucket, I cleared my throat as if I were going to make an important announcement.

'I know why your name's Ms Bucket.'

'Why is that, Lisa?'

I giggled. 'Because you look like a bucket.' And in her long pink skirt she did.

Her face froze.

'That is very rude and not a very nice thing for a little girl to say. Don't ever say that again. I think you need to say you're sorry.'

My long piggy tails, which were pulled neatly in place with bottle-green baubles and thick satin ribbons tied in perfect bows, slid down my chest.

'I...I'm sorry.'

My confident voice faded to a pathetic whimper. I didn't

like getting into trouble. And to think just a few minutes earlier I was the one in charge of who was allowed in and out of the cubby house. I was a natural leader, or *Miss Bossy Boots,* as one of the kids called me. I was certainly not a follower. Maybe it wasn't the most polite thing to say, but I was five, and it was my first day of school. And it was true.

As far as I can recall, that was the moment I started becoming a goody-goody and began to be kneaded smaller, constricted from the contours of my inner truth.

At home, I often felt out of place.

'You're not even part of the family,' Kim would tell me.

'What do you mean?'

'Haven't you noticed that Mum, Dad and I all have greeny-blue eyes and yours are all browny?'

My eyes froze wide.

'You were adopted,' she would tell me all matter-of-factly. 'Look at your ski-jump nose. It's different to all of our straight ones. Ha ha ha ha!'

With my chin to my chest, I placed my pointer finger between my eyebrows and traced a line down to the tip of my nose. Kim's squinty eyes poked out from behind her dead-straight fringe and the tips of her fingers, her hands concealing her laughter. I was desperate to know I belonged to my family. The thought that I may not, made me tearful. Was I the ugly duckling of our clan?

As kids, we used to crush cans with Dad's gigantic mallet and swap them for money. Insidiously, I began, in the same way, to squash who I was. I learnt to copy other family members. Instead of displaying my confidence, I recoiled introspectively. Instead of exploring my vivid imagination, I clung to facts. I had to be more like the people I wanted to like me. *If I wasn't, I wouldn't belong, would I?*

I checked my status with Mum. 'Kim is just being a troublemaker and stirring you up,' she assured me.

'Yeah, I knew that,' I said, letting out a balloon-sized breath.

I needed to belong to feel worthy.

Early on, I became interested in spirituality; but Mum, Dad and Kim didn't share my curiosity. From an early age I had a sense that I was being guided by some higher power. In Dad's parents' home, on the dressing table in my Aunty Linda's old room, stood a one-metre-high statue of Jesus wearing a red cape. Its eyes seemed to follow me wherever I went, while from the picture rail alongside the bed hung a haloed picture of Jesus who stared down on me. In my mind, the statue and picture of Jesus held me close to something bigger.

In the following years, my need for connection crossed over into my school life. I craved acceptance from the other kids. Apart from our academic performance, isn't that the crux of our childhood angst? Issues with friends. Not feeling included. Not being 'in' on the joke.

Sometimes I wasn't allowed to do after-school activities with the other kids if Mum and Dad thought it was dangerous, or there was no supervision. Other times I was the one who said no. Without realising it, I began to exclude myself from group activities and, in the process, missed opportunities to connect with my schoolmates. When you are absent, others develop bonds, and you lose out on forging. You get left behind.

When I was twelve, I once asked Mum if I could go roller skating with my friend Rebecca.

'What, just the two of you?'

'I think there may be a few others going, but she goes all the time.'

'You don't even know how to skate.'

'Yeah, but it'll be fun. I'll learn.'

'I don't think it's a good idea. Are her parents going?'

'They drop her off. It's fine. You can drop me off and pick me up inside.' I pleaded with a long and drawn-out 'please.' 'Everyone else is allowed to do stuff. Why can't I ever do anything?'

'I don't care if everyone else is going. *You're* not.'

I begged her until she gave in. 'Oh, all right then, but don't come crying to me when you've hurt yourself.'

On the rink, I felt like a superstar as I shuffled around the edge, not straying too far from the safety rail. As I built my confidence, I swooshed out amongst the professional skaters. Olivia Newton-John in *Xanadu* flashed before me. Reach and glide, reach and glide. I was in time with the beat.

And then my eagerness got ahead of me. As I lurched forward, I felt my skates sliding out from underneath me. As the shiny concrete rose up to meet me, both quickly and slowly, I extended my arms to protect my body. My left arm took the weight of the fall. I was in agony.

Later at the hospital I asked Mum, 'Will it get better?'

A bone in my wrist was sticking up three centimetres out of place. Mum looked at me with pursed lips. She didn't say, '*I told you so,*' but her eyes screamed it. I spent six weeks in a half cast to fix my greenstick fracture.

All this accident did was reinforce my conditioning: when

Mum and Dad warned me something bad would happen, it would. They were right. *Goddamn it, they were always right.* It cemented my belief that their word was gospel and I stopped trusting my own judgement. If Mum and Dad didn't agree with me, I would decide against my own opinion even if I thought it was the right thing to do. During this important time in the development of my personality, I learned not to trust my adventurous spirit, and instead, conformed even more.

Of course, Mum and Dad were just trying to protect me. Parents generally know better. They dissuaded me from taking risks to assuage their fears about my safety. But in cushioning me against making mistakes, I lost the learning as well as the fall. Only later did my lessons come, but they were bigger and harder than if I'd learnt them when I was young.

Being a curious child, I once turned the playground microphone on at recess when I was in Year Two. I wanted to know how the rectangular box speaker worked. It was the size of a gym punching bag. How could it make Mrs Forster's voice so loud it reached all edges of the playground? I flicked the button, which resulted in a loud, high-pitched and very annoying sound. Everyone's eyes were on me. Mrs Forster marched over and sent me to detention.

'You are not to touch the microphone. You can stay here until recess is over and think about what you have done.'

My eyes struggled to meet hers.

I was mortified that I'd gotten into trouble. I was only trying to see how the microphone worked. But I was so ashamed that I never again got into strife at school.

At home, Kim and I had to do what we were told or suffer

the consequences: we were grounded, sent to our rooms or denied dessert. Those early years became my foundation, and they sent me further away from my soul.

Being a girl came with added restrictions, especially as I became a teenager.

As boys started flirting, I pretended I wasn't interested. I'd seen Dad get angry at Kim when she'd brought boys over without asking him or Mum if it was okay. I wasn't going to cause any trouble. I never had any teenage relationships.

Years of this behaviour caused me to protect myself in the same way that growth rings form layers on a tree trunk. Many years later, I would need to chip away at these to release my true self.

I relied on everyone else to direct the course of my life. I never developed my own instincts. When the time came to make my own choices, I was a novice.

Unsurprisingly, this led me to make some shocking decisions in the coming years.

3

CHEATING BOYFRIEND

Before Adrian, there was Scott.

'When is Lisa going to get a boyfriend?' I once overheard one of the grandparents saying to Mum and Dad.

'She doesn't seem interested,' Mum said.

'Maybe she doesn't like men?' Nanna said.

I was getting to the age where if you'd never had a boyfriend, there was something *wrong*. So when the first decent young man asked me out, I said yes. His name was Scott.

I started dating Scott, a work colleague, when I was twenty-one. I only went on a date with him because he liked me. He was polite and kind, so why not? But truthfully, I wasn't attracted to him.

'How's it going with Scott?' My friend Belinda asked after

Scott and I had a few dates.

It was difficult to speak openly because back in the nineties, our phone was attached to the wall in a common area of the house. I wasn't comfortable having the family overhear a conversation about my first experience with a boy.

'Okay. We had a nice dinner last night. I keep thinking it's good, then I think, he's not for me, then he's really nice, I'm not sure. He's not a murderer or a thief – put it that way. I suppose I'll just see how it goes.'

Belinda laughed at how low the bar of my ridiculously high standards had fallen. I had always imagined I would meet a man who would fall madly in love with me and sweep me off my feet. All the media I'd been exposed to had confirmed this. What were the alternatives? It wasn't an option to remain single or be in a same-sex relationship. Conversations about the future were always couched in outdated fairy tale scenarios, and the assumption that every young woman would grow up, get married and have a family.

Scott and I had fun together. We enjoyed watching movies and loved those lazy Sunday mornings when 'reading the papers' was a thing. We were both family people and regularly spent time with both sets of parents.

One Sunday almost two years into our relationship, Scott came to visit while I was still living with Mum and Dad. He was distracted. I couldn't work out why. After a couple of hours, he seemed eager to leave.

'Catch you later,' Scott said to Mum and Dad in the lounge room. He gave them an open-handed wave. I couldn't help noticing how dirty and stained the crevices of his palm were.

Worker's hands, I called them. He worked in the produce department at a supermarket, so it was understandable. His eyes found the floor and a muscle was twitching in his jaw.

It was the day Princess Diana passed away. I'd spent the morning in the family room, snuggled into the pink-and-blue cane recliner – Dad's seat on a Saturday afternoon when he listened to the horse races – watching the depressing coverage on TV.

I followed Scott out the front door, to the slate porch.

'I need to…a-ahem. I, um, need to talk to you.'

We sat on the top step. Through my pants, I felt the coolness of the tiles.

There was silence.

'Uh, I got a little drunk last night at the club…and…'

'And?' My eyes were trying to extract the words. 'What is it? What are you trying to say?'

There was no reason to, but I stood up.

'Um, I kinda kissed someone, that's all.'

'You what?' *I must have heard wrong.*

'I know. I don't know what to say.'

'How do you kind of –'

'I know, I know. I'm stupid and shouldn't have done it, but I love you. I love you so much. I really do. I'm sorry. I didn't know what I was doing. I had to tell you. It's burning me up. You *have* to forgive me.'

His tone grated on me, like a kid begging for ice cream. *Please, Mum. Can I? Can I?* My body felt separate from me. *This can't be happening.* I was already so sad about Princess Diana. Numb.

It turns out he'd kissed someone I knew, a woman I used to work with at my weekend job. My stomach felt as if it was being wrung like a dishcloth.

'I think it's best if you go.'

'I'll never do it again. You can trust me. I made a mistake. You have to forgive me.'

He put his arms around me. I was a sandstone block.

What was everyone going to say when they found out?

He managed a wry smile as he stepped off the pebblecrete path. How could someone so guilt-ridden look so virtuous?

After he'd driven off, I took a deep breath and went back inside. The grief on the TV was easier to deal with than Scott's infidelity. I had delayed dating until my twenties and had wanted our relationship to be perfect. I was so ashamed I had been cheated on. I know it was only a kiss, but it seemed like such a betrayal. *Maybe because he was my first?*

I didn't tell anyone.

I didn't want Mum and Dad to judge Scott or think less of him. They liked him and thought he was funny. He was always doing or saying something clumsy. I sensed they didn't think we were compatible or see a long-term future for us. (Mum confirmed my suspicions once we'd broken up.)

I was used to putting on a brave face. *Don't upset the apple cart. Pretend everything is okay. They'll just think I'm sad about Princess Di.* My unrealistic expectations of my fantasy prince died on the same day that a real-life princess had. Like a song that takes you to a time in the past, I can't think of either of these events without the other.

The next morning, as I waited for my train to work, after

holding it all in at home, I cried. It didn't matter. The mood was sombre, faces downturned to the concrete platform. On the train, passengers were reading newspapers. One of the headlines read, 'DI DEAD.' My tears were safely hidden amongst the collective mourning.

I didn't want to confess Scott's sin because not only would everyone think differently of him, but they would also think differently of me. I pretended it didn't happen. That way, I could protect myself from having to admit that I didn't have the perfect life with the perfect boyfriend.

But I was already adept at pretending. I'd practised the art of hiding as a kid when we watched sad movies, forcing myself not to cry. I'd feel my heart beating in my throat, but I wouldn't let the tears flow. I'd look straight at the television, grit my teeth and avoid eye contact with my family. Mum and Dad were always straight-faced, modelling how to be strong and tough. It was one of those unwritten rules of our family. I saved my tears for when I wanted attention or if I was being sooky. On these occasions, Dad would say, 'Stop being such a baby.' Being emotional felt like a form of weakness, so I learnt to hold those big feelings in. I'd wait till I went to bed and then release the floodgates on my pillow. That water-stained pillow knew the real me.

Well done to me. I had deceived everyone again. I didn't look out of place on the train that day. I could pretend my sadness was about Princess Di, not about Scott kissing another woman at Club Troppo.

But then I did something even worse. I wondered what Scott's betrayal said about me. *Why wasn't I enough for him?* I even felt sorry for him. Of course, I forgave him and acted as if his actions hadn't affected me. I didn't open up to Mum and Dad, who may have guided me towards my truth. I was afraid they'd tell me I deserved better, which was what I needed to hear. To make matters worse, Scott's mum, Mandy, then took on the role of spokesperson, begging me for forgiveness on his behalf.

'He loves you so much, darlin. It was just the alcohol. He didn't mean it. *Please* forgive him. He won't do it again.'

She wasn't to know that would end up being a lie.

And godhelpme, I stayed with Scott for five more years.

The night Scott and I moved into the unit we'd saved long and hard for, we invited his parents over with two other couples we'd just met for a celebration barbecue. We were proud to purchase our first piece of real estate. At some point, Scott's mum began to tap her elbow repeatedly against Scott's arm like a chicken trying to take flight. Her tongue was pressed firmly into her cheek before she whispered – loud enough for me to hear, 'Now that you have your own place, why don't you ask Lisa to marry you? Go on.' She shooed him towards me with both hands. 'It's about time.'

Scott was laughing nervously and swallowing hard. 'Lisa… will you…uh…marry me?'

It stumbled out like a ninety-year-old trying to jump hurdles.

I waited for everyone to laugh. But it clearly wasn't a joke. All eyes were on me. Mine were burning. His dad nodded his head expectantly. He was waiting for the *yes*. I'd always imagined a tender, private moment anywhere but on the balcony having a barbecue with shiny new friends and parents gawking at us.

If Scott needed his mother to prompt him, how was he going to be my man, my rock, a father to my children... someone to lean on?

I paused before I said, 'Not if you're going to ask me like that.'

His mum was first to speak.

'It'll never happen. You two are never gonna get married.' She stomped inside. 'I'm going to bed.'

She waved one hand above her head as she walked upstairs.

As the mood changed, our new neighbours soon left. At least we had given them a story to tell. Scott sulked off to bed.

Before that night, I'd always assumed we would marry. Scott was polite, considerate and seemed to genuinely love me. We had fun times together. Why had I reacted so vehemently to the proposal? It made me question, for the first time, if our relationship was enough for me. *If I had wanted to marry him, wouldn't I have said yes, no matter the circumstances?*

Then it hit me – I wanted more – though I'd never thought about what that 'more' was.

Why hadn't I thought about it? I had no vision or direction for my own life. Suddenly, I felt stuck; and like a reflex, I switched on my bedside lamp and yanked open the top drawer of my bedside table to double-check I'd taken my pill that day. I didn't want to take the chance of falling pregnant and getting trapped here.

I woke restlessly several times that night as my mind jumped from thought to thought. Instead of remembering the good times, the picnics at Hardy's Bay, the driving holidays and dinners at local restaurants, I began to stack the negative memories one on top of each other, like the mattresses in *The Princess and the Pea*. I'd always harboured a niggling feeling that he wasn't the right man for me, but I'd hoped they would magically disappear if I buried the little pea under enough excuses.

I knew I'd honoured myself saying no to Scott's mother-in-law-induced proposal.

Though I seemed to make choices to please others, keep the peace or protect other people's feelings, funnily enough, I always had the strength to say no when it really mattered.

Scott was my first experience of love. All up, I stayed with him for seven years.

The biggest surprise of all is how our relationship ended.

4

CHEATING SELF

In between Scott and Adrian was Todd – the relationship I'd pressed Command + x on, for the same reason I would leave a job off my resume. I was not proud of it – it always felt like that one moment that could ruin my reputation were it to get out.

'Are you sure about this, Lisa?' Todd asked.

Scott and I hadn't officially separated, but our breakup felt imminent.

'I'm sure,' I said.

Even though it was dark, the suffocating peach interior of that hotel room is etched in my memory. The paint. The curtains. The cushions.

Todd could have been a politician; he was so charming. Our attraction was initiated by a seductive stroke on my arm while I was typing at work. You know the soft area above the back of your elbow? An electric current ran up my spine to the nape of my neck when he ran his finger ever…so…gently over my skin. Scott's touch never made me feel this way. I didn't realise at the time that Todd did this to all the women in the office. For him, it was a numbers game. Eventually, someone would respond to his advances.

'I totally understand. I'm going through the same thing with my girlfriend.' Todd had told me when I'd verbalised my frustration at being in limbo in my relationship with Scott.

'We're going to sell our house to make it final,' he'd added.

I'd confided that Scott and I were also considering selling our co-owned unit.

We bonded over our apparent mutual sorrow. Todd was everything Scott wasn't: playful, cheeky, irresponsible and a rule breaker – a perfect rebound candidate with whom I could explore my devilish side. I'd been playing the goody-goody all my life and suddenly, here was my chance to rebel. I didn't think about a future with Todd, just how much I wanted him to rip my clothes off. It was sheer lust. When he asked if I was sure that night in the hotel, I said yes without hesitation.

I'd had so little experience with dating. Throughout my teens, I'd automatically said no to anyone who showed interest in me. It was easier. No wonder I associated sex with being 'bad.' All I'd been taught was that it was not allowed, and from my teenage perspective, sex was 'naughty.' I didn't want to be dirty, slutty or cheap – words I'd heard associated with youthful relationships. Good girls weren't supposed to have sex, let alone enjoy it.

I was exhilarated by what Todd brought out in me. Being free to express my sexuality opened something inside me that previously I'd been afraid to explore. The thrill of being caught having sex in a car, or someone catching us while we were sneaking around, added to the excitement.

'Quick, duck,' Todd said.

We hid below the dashboard when we saw a car's headlights approaching us at one of our secret rendezvous spots.

How we laughed. Not that anyone would have seen us through the foggy windows.

Once I'd had to wear high neck skivvies and scarves when I stayed with Kim, embarrassed at the bruises on my neck, but exhilarated at how they'd gotten there.

I was making up for the time I'd lost, relishing having someone who wanted to devour me. I'd started to let go of my old-fashioned conditioning and realised that experimenting with my sexuality was a natural part of life, not a punishable sin. We were consumed with unrestrained desire for each other. For several months, neither of us broke up with our partners. The truth was we were both cheating on them.

Emotionally, I had already broken up with Scott, but we were still financially tied and living together. I wondered whether my affair with Todd was my way of exacting revenge for the hurt and betrayal he'd inflicted on me all those years ago. Had I ever really forgiven him for kissing someone else? I couldn't tell him about Todd. I never did. I had convinced myself that he would be too heartbroken, but really, I couldn't bear how ashamed I was. I felt as though I had tarnished my reputation forever.

I only went back to Scott's bed once after being with Todd, and I cried the entire time. I knew I couldn't stay. I knew I had to end it. I was just prolonging the pain for everyone. In trying to avoid inflicting pain on Scott, I'd made things far worse. It wasn't fair on him. I gathered up the courage.

'Hey, I need to talk to you about something.'

'What?'

'It's just that – ah – when we sell, I don't want to live with you anymore.'

'Huh?' Scott looked confused.

It was hard for me to look at him.

'It's not about you, it's me. I'm just not happy.'

I had practised this goddamn conversation for months, but it came as a complete shock to him.

'I can't *believe* this. Don't you…love me anymore?'

'Of course, I love you. I'm just not *in* love with you anymore. It's pretty obvious that I haven't been happy, isn't it?'

We hadn't slept together in months. That should have been a fair indicator.

'We can work this out,' he said.

'There's nothing to work out. I've thought a lot about this.'

My legs kept tensing and rising in spasms, as if I was in a dentist's chair. *What was he going to say? What was he going to do?*

'It sounds like you have.' Scott flung his hands in the air before walking away, leaving me alone. Even though I felt like vomiting, I took my first deep breath in a while.

I was inexperienced at breaking up and appreciated for the first time why people stay in ill-fated relationships to avoid heartache. I thought it was weakness that stopped people from leaving. But in that moment, I understood that it's possible to want to end a relationship but still stay to avoid the hurt to yourself and others.

After several more conversations with Scott, he accepted we were over.

'I can't stay here with you if we aren't together.'

'I really am sorry.'

He gave me a cheeky smile and hugged me. 'I don't agree, but I know I can't change your mind.'

'Thank you. I hope we can still be friends.'

Scott went to stay with his parents, and I remained in our home until we found a buyer. We completed a sale a few months later.

'I really never thought this would happen,' Scott said.

I packed my trinkets into the boxes we'd lined up. It was horrible to see the beautiful home we'd created come down to blank walls and boxes with either 'Lisa' or 'Scott' written in thick black marker.

When I saw the sheer pain on his face and the tears in his eyes, I couldn't help but cry. I'd never broken up with anyone before. We'd had some great times. We loved each other, but I wasn't fulfilled. I had to experience more of my life and not just settle down with Scott because it was expected after we'd been together for so long.

I then rented a granny flat, and Scott bought another property with his half of the proceeds of the sale.

One day after Scott and I separated, Todd's ex, Louise, called the office and I answered the phone. She wanted to let him know he'd forgotten his lunch. 'Tell him I'll bring it in for him,' she said. The loving tone in her voice didn't make sense. I shook my head. I hadn't given her a thought because Todd had assured me they were finished.

Suddenly, I realised she had no idea what we'd been up to in the previous months.

I felt sick with guilt.

Even though no-one was watching, I blushed as I hung up the phone. Todd confirmed my fears. I felt sick knowing I had both annihilated my own morals and inadvertently affected the life of an innocent person – a lovely woman with whom I could have easily been friends under different circumstances. This fact alone was debilitating. I could not look in the mirror without berating myself. *How could you do this to someone?*

After that, I stayed home and retreated into myself. I continued to have pains in my stomach. I believed it was a punishment I deserved.

Several nights later, Todd knocked violently on my screen door. He'd been out with his mates. I refused to open it.

'It's so cold out here and I've had too many drinks. I can't drive home,' Todd begged from the other side. 'Please, let me in.'

'You'll have to sleep in your car then. I'm not letting you in. You lied to me. You said you were leaving too. Don't even think about coming back while you're still with her,' I shouted.

Todd turned and walked away without looking back. I closed the curtain.

That night, I cried into the scarf that Scott's mum had knitted for me the previous winter. Sometimes the seasons of our life have a peculiar way of overlapping. I was trembling, but

I left Todd to sleep in his car. It was the heart of winter, and I didn't even offer him a blanket. I was relieved at my resolve.

But the shame of what I'd put myself and Louise through became a secret I never wanted anyone to find out about.

My body took the toll. I got an upset tummy. I lost weight, and had persistent diarrhoea, insomnia and outbreaks of skin rashes. My body was attempting to get my attention.

A cloud of shame clung to me like a shadow.

A few months later, I heard Todd's familiar knock on the screen door.

'I've left her,' Todd declared.

'What?'

'You told me that while I'm still with her, we can't be together, so I left her.'

No. This was not happening. I had never thought he would break up with Louise for me. I thought I was free. *Shit.*

But I'd made the terms; now I had to honour them. I felt responsible for the whole mess.

And so I let Todd move in. I know, I know.

Once we were living together, the real Todd showed up. He couldn't pay his rent. I suddenly saw clearly what had always been in front of me: Todd was a compulsive gambler, chain-smoker and heavy drinker. He would make a beeline to the poker machines after receiving each pay, which was why he kept borrowing money from me, racking up an IOU of ten thousand dollars. I imagined with him moving in, I'd get it back quicker as he no longer had to pay his own rent. Instead, it just gave him more money to gamble with.

'I need eight hundred and fifty dollars. They're going to

come and collect my car right now if I don't pay straight away,' he'd beg.

He appeared distraught, and I fell for it each time. From a young age, I had been taught to be financially independent and had always been extra careful with my money – I still had all the profits I won playing marbles in Year Six, if you can believe. Even my boss had loaned Todd money several times after his relentless begging. In hindsight, I suspect Todd had targeted me when he heard I was selling my house and imagined I'd have cash to fuel his addictions. And this was how I let myself be buried deeper in the Todd hole.

It's hard to comprehend why I sacrificed my deepest intuitions out of guilt. Again. I guess once I had made the mistake, it felt too late. I couldn't take it all back. I dwelled on my foolishness and beat myself up incessantly. The perfectionist in me hadn't learnt how important and inevitable mistakes are for human development. I felt I'd failed myself as well as my parents. The weight of the guilt was heavy and overwhelming, and I found it impossible to see or think clearly.

A few more months passed, I noticed Todd was more interested in drinking with his mates than spending time with me. One day he grabbed my upper arm really hard.

'You weren't talking to another man, were you?' he said through tightly clenched teeth.

He squeezed my humerus bone between his thumb and fingers. It felt like he was threatening me, showing me what he was capable of if I didn't act the way he wanted.

The next day, a golf-ball-sized bruise appeared.

And that was a line crossed I was never going to tolerate. I saw his jealousy and I didn't find it charming. It was frightening. I recognised I was in the wrong place.

I still let Christmas, then his birthday and Valentine's Day pass. But I'd planned an overseas trip with a friend, and I wanted him out before I left.

When I told Todd he had to leave, he glared at me, called me a fucking c*** and strolled out the door without looking back.

I eventually recouped my money from him in increments over several years due to my sheer insistence and persistence. I felt a wonderful sense of satisfaction when the last cent was paid back.

We all have something we'd rather not share, but without revealing all facets of who we are, we are only showing part of the story and not being true and authentic. Keeping our shames hidden is what gives them power over us. It took more than a decade for me to forgive myself, but I am now free of the weighty guilt I've carried.

My relationship with Todd gave me invaluable dating experience that I hadn't had as a teenager. Who knows where I'd be if Todd hadn't come into my life to unsettle things? Maybe I would have married my first boyfriend without ever experiencing another relationship.

Once he was gone, I was genuinely relieved to be on my own. My next relationship was going to have to be with someone interested in living a healthy lifestyle like I was committed to. If not, I pledged to remain single. And one thing was for sure – they had to be a non-smoker. Even twenty years later, if I catch the slightest waft of cigarette smoke, it immediately takes me back to those terrible times.

Todd also taught me a swift lesson in judgement. I knew I was behaving wrongly, but I did it anyway. Having gone through with it, I know with certainty I'd never dishonour myself in that way again. I could never have said that until I had lived through the emotions and the consequences my decision unleashed. When we think we are above a certain type of behaviour, the universe has a way of bringing us into equilibrium. I shouldn't have been surprised that I found myself doing exactly what I'd judged other people for. I shouldn't have been surprised that I discovered a kinder understanding in myself after this ordeal.

I wish I hadn't gotten involved with Todd in the first place, but I only see now how the relationship served a greater purpose: to get me out of the rut I was in, to move my life forward. I needed to learn through living.

I had six wonderful months on my own before I met Adrian. Although I went into my third relationship knowing what I didn't want, I was still living a watered-down version of myself in all aspects of my life, including my work.

I was in a sales-administration role in a real-estate office on the Central Coast of New South Wales. I'd wanted to become an agent but had convinced myself I didn't have the personality for it. Seven years had flown by. I'd only taken the job as a fill in when I left a great position in Sydney as a resort conference sales executive. I left because of the four hours a day commute. That's what I claimed anyway. The truth was, I was anxious and uncomfortable speaking up in meetings and in front of the bosses. The job was demanding more interaction with and entertainment of clients. My fears had taken over. I craved safety like a child clutching a beloved soft toy. In the real-estate office, I could work away in the background without attracting too much attention.

I kept avoiding the signs and was only seeing what was on the surface. I was still oblivious to the extent of the manipulation and treatment I'd accepted from men. I didn't know at the time, but the voice of the universe was about to get much louder. Then I'd have no other choice but to take notice of the flashing neon signs and finally wake up.

5
───────

WARPED VALUES

One day, when I was in Year Three, I was showing off my new pencil box which closed with the click of a magnet to my friend, Lesley. They were the craze at the time. Kim and I always got the latest things.

'Look, each section is a different shape so the pencils, pens, erasers and sharpeners have their own spots. It costs fifteen dollars,' I said proudly.

'Why do you always have to say the price?' she asked.

I didn't mean to – but I always just blurted out what things cost. In our home, Mum treated objects with great value. I simply copied what I was taught and, without realising it, tended to acknowledge it out loud.

One afternoon Kim and I spotted Mum and Dad in the

garage. It looked like they were both crying.

'I don't remember *ever* seeing Dad cry,' I said. 'This must be really bad.'

As we approached them, we saw that the new metallic blue Celica had a huge scratch down one side of it as if it had been dented with a trolley. They were devastated. I was confused. They didn't show emotion when they were sad, but here they were, crying over a scratch on the car. Material things clearly meant a great deal to them.

When we were little, we had to save everything for later. But when was later?

Kim and I had an extensive collection of novelty erasers trapped on display in a clear plastic jar. Sometimes we'd spread them out over the kitchen floor to count, categorize or just sniff their sweet, perfumed rubber. We never thought about using them for their intended purpose. There was no need. We didn't make enough mistakes to warrant their use.

Candles were also only for display. Once they were lit, they were 'ruined.' The 'good' dinner set and glasses were for special occasions. We had to learn to drive in Dad's company ute, not the family car, in case we damaged it. I saved special stationery too, never writing letters which would 'waste' the paper. Sometimes, if I had heaps of the same kind, I would write a secret letter on one sheet. Years later, I threw all the ornate stationery in the bin as it had become discoloured with yellowy brown spots. I wished I had used it all up as a kid and sent my thoughts on adventures through the post.

These were generational values. Mum and Dad, and baby boomers like them, grew up in households of frugality. Their parents had lived through the war and the Depression, when things were scarce and rationed; and people *had* to hold onto everything to reuse – rubber bands, wrapping paper, string, buttons. People hoarded and stocked up for the hard times. Pop collected every nail, bolt or screw he found and separated them into rusty tins in the garage. Mum remembers him saying, 'I'll find a use for that.' She detested his habit of washing and reusing freezer bags because they smelt like dirty dishrags.

I remember Nanna, Mum's mum, making us stay seated at the dinner table until we finished every morsel of food.

'Don't leave the table until your plate is clean.'

Food was never thrown in the bin.

Mum often tells the story of how she threw the metal suitcase her dad made for her for school down the street to try to break it so she could get a new one, but it was indestructible. She made up for those lean early years later in her life, by having whatever she wanted to excess.

Dad built our split-level home on the Central Coast of New South Wales, where we lived for my primary school years. It seemed huge compared to my friends' houses. Until we were teenagers, Kim and I shared a bedroom and used the spare room as our playroom. Two old wooden wardrobes held the treasures of our childhood. Large, old-fashioned keys stuck out of the locks. The wood was splitting and looked like it could fall apart, but we didn't care. We were only interested in what was inside. Mouse Trap, KerPlunk, I Took a Lickin' from a Chicken, The Tree Tots Family Tree House, Hungry Hungry Hippos, Lite-Brite, Fuzzy Pumpers and, of course, Monopoly, Scrabble, Boggle and an endless sea of Lego.

We were spoilt with a collection of Nintendo Game & Watch handheld games we called *dit dits* because of the sounds they made. Our friends were lucky to own one or two, but we had more than ten. We knew they were expensive because Mum often reminded us. We kept score of the current champion of each game in a spiral-bound notebook. I was the *Turtle Bridge* champ. No-one else could be bothered trying to beat my record. When we had finished playing, we always returned them to the hard foam packaging and slid them back in the box they came in.

We also had dozens of dolls. I collected Strawberry Shortcakes and Kim had Baby Alive, but I was desperate for a Barbie. I recall flicking through the pages of the Casey's Toyworld catalogue one night before falling asleep, and in the morning handing Mum a list of *My Favourite Barbies*. I had a Sindy doll, but Sindy didn't cut it. She wasn't Barbie. Kim had a Barbie, but a boring one. It had an old-fashioned hairdo that looked like Nanna's – all curly and short. No fun at all. We couldn't even comb her hair.

Each Christmas, Santa left individual and shared presents for me and Kim. The shared ones were usually board games. Whenever we saw a card that said *To Kim and Lisa*, we'd fight to rip the paper off and be the first to see. One year, it was a Barbie. Pink and Pretty. My flushed, freckly face could have burst and we hadn't even opened the box.

Mum always said she and Dad spoilt us because she wasn't allowed to have toys or fun things when she was growing up. She wanted us to have the things she missed out on.

With all this excess, Kim and I once found ourselves

in school holidays draped over the suede kitchen stools, complaining to Mum.

'I'm bored. What can we do?' I asked.

'You've *got* to be kidding,' Mum said. 'You have a whole room full of toys up there. Go and play, or do your latch hook, or play with the Atari. You *must* be able to find *something* to do. If you can't find anything, iron the hankies or unpack the dishwasher.' We were never trusted with ironing actual clothes. It was always the hankies or tea towels.

Suddenly, we weren't bored. We ran up to the playroom and opened the cupboard doors. Lying on the floor, arms behind our heads, Kim rested her feet on the corner of the cupboard door; and I leant mine against the wall.

'Twister?' I asked.

'That's boring with only two of us.'

'What about Headache or Trouble?'

'Nah, they take too long.'

'What about Barbies?'

'Let's play schools. My Barbie will be the teacher, and Sindy and Pink and Pretty can be the kids,' Kim suggested.

I held on to Pink and Pretty's long legs and swung her around so her hair fanned out. She looked like the main character from the TV show, *I Dream of Jeannie*, with the little bit of hair wrapped around her high ponytail. A few years after we'd first opened the box, the tiny rubber bands tucked underneath still held the shiny hair perfectly in place.

'It's not fair,' I moaned to Kim. 'No-one else has to keep the hair left up.'

'You know we're not allowed. We'll get in trouble.'

'Mum would get so cranky, wouldn't she?'

We could always smell the fun, but we weren't allowed to taste it.

'I'm going to ask Santa for one of those Barbie Styling Head dolls that are just a head on a stand,' I told Kim. 'Then I could plait, brush or comb for as long as I want. That's what they're for. Belinda has one, and when I go over there, we do all different styles. There are heaps of ties, clips and ribbons. It's the best.'

Even though I loved inventing new styles with my own long hair, I wore it in the same half-up pony style in every single school photo from kindy to the end of primary school. Seven years in a row. One day in Year Four, as I walked to school with my neighbour Karmel, I stopped dead when she said, 'We won't be doing much today. Half the day will be taken up with school photos.'

I panicked. I ran back home in a flap. My day's ponytail wasn't going to suffice. Mum patiently redid my hair for me in the traditional style. As I walked back to school, flustered, I felt relieved that Karmel had reminded me it was photo day. I never felt in control unless everything – including my hair – was in place.

I know why I was anxious about my appearance. It came from my family's tendency to judge and criticize the way people looked.

At night, we'd sit around watching TV, examining the actors' appearances as if we were scoring them in a pageant.

'Oh, look how much she's aged.'

'Check out that hairstyle.'

'Nice outfit…he he.'

'How did he get on TV? He has a perfect face for radio.'

Though I participated in judging others to fit in, I was secretly terrified of becoming the subject of this kind of scrutiny, so I began to guard my essence like the Holy Grail. I was afraid I'd be found lacking because – as much as I tried – I knew I wasn't perfect. As a result, I was painfully conscious of how I looked all throughout my childhood.

I learned this from Mum who never left the house without being done up with neat hair, freshly ironed clothes and conservative make-up with only brown-toned lipsticks because the pigment in her skin turned pink shades to bright red. To keep her hair in place, she has always avoided windy situations – which means she has always avoided weather.

I copied her and would fret if anyone came over to the house before I was ready.

'Lisa, Vicki's at the door. She wants to know if you can babysit tonight.'

'Just a minute,' I would yell from my bedroom. I'd throw on clothes, half-brush my hair, and slap on face powder and mascara. God forbid if Vicki caught sight of me in my pyjamas with a red face. *Argh, I should have woken up earlier.* As a result, no-one got to see the natural Lisa.

In high school, they ran a buddy system called *Peer Support*, where a group of Year Eleven students were selected to assist the Year Seven students with their transition into high school. But I got my period the day before the annual camp, so I made up some excuse about why I couldn't go. I stepped down and allowed someone else to take my place. I cried about that. I wanted to be a role model and felt I'd let my Year Seven kids down. But my fear of having a menstrual accident won out. I could never face going beyond my comfort zone.

I craved certainty in all areas of my life and avoided putting myself in situations where I wasn't in control of the outcome.

Looking back on my childhood, I can see how many of my formative years I spent valuing the wrong things. It seemed innocent back then.

But it primed me for later on in life, when I'd come to value all the wrong men.

6

MOTHERING MAN-BOYS

'Too heavy,' I'd groan if Adrian tried to spoon me in bed.

The pressure of the weight of his arm across my body as he relaxed into sleep constricted my breathing. I would pivot his bent arm at the shoulder joint like a Ken doll until it was back by his side.

'Sorry. It's squashing me.'

'Ha. Hmmm.' He would chuckle with self-satisfaction in his sleepy garble.

We had ourselves a win-win situation. The weight of his enormous upper limbs, the result of hours at the gym, gave me an excuse to have my own space, and he got to feel dominant and mighty. Despite their size, I never once felt safe inside his arms. He always made me feel less.

Once he asked me, 'Do you think Jack is bigger than me?' He was referring to his muscles. He wanted to be seen as the king of the gym jungle. Extra muscles are also a great way to silently dominate.

Truthfully, his friend was double his size.

'He has put a little bit of size on recentl—' I tried, diplomatically.

'Yeah? Well, you're not *even* at competition level,' Adrian interrupted. The ferocity of his tone made my stomach flinch.

'I never said I wanted to be at competition level. I go to the gym for my health and to be fit. When did I ever say anything about competing?'

'Well, you couldn't if you tried.'

Then I'd receive the silent treatment as punishment.

Adrian would look at his reflection in every shiny surface. He always sought reassurance about superficial things.

'How does my hair look?'

'Do I look big in this?'

He made sure to mention that one of his ex's breasts were like a model's – whatever that means. He always updated me on how much weight his past girlfriends had put on.

'She's never looked as good as when she was with me.'

He routinely put all women down.

'The next prime minister might be a woman,' I once said hopefully as I watched the news.

'Ha. That will never happen. Not in my lifetime anyway.'

I had a chuckle to myself a few years later when Julia Gillard became the first female prime minister of Australia in 2010.

As I matured, I grew out of thinking that people 'had

faces for radio' and I had to be 'ready' before anyone saw me. As my relationship with Adrian fell apart, instead of me gaining confidence, I became more insecure. I always took his comments as veiled threats warning me that without him, I'd get fat and ugly.

Deep insecurities are always rooted in pain. I knew Adrian was protecting himself from rejection, but that way of being began to spill over into my life. I was drained and hurt by the constant game-playing. His words stung, reflecting my own critical sense of self.

I'd always thought of myself as an honest person, but was this, in fact, true? Had I been trained, like Pavlov's dogs, to anticipate particular responses and say what other people wanted to hear to avoid negative reactions? *Was I scared to tell the truth?*

Author and internationally renowned motivational speaker, Mel Robbins, reveals in her book, *The High 5 Habit*, how people pleasers are liars. She believes we will say anything so that others see us as 'good' because we are motivated by trying not to upset anyone.

Precedence had created a terrible pattern in which I'd been embarrassed or punished whenever I told the truth. I became an expert in telling lies. *Why don't I just say how it is?* I often wondered.

I needed to stop being a child.

It was time to face the truth about my relationships with men so I could start to tell the truth.

Adrian always gave the impression that he was overflowing with confidence. But when he lost his job, three years into our relationship, he cowered in the foetal position and hid from the world. Horrible memories return when I think of it.

He made it clear that losing his job was my problem, and the overwhelming financial burden became my responsibility. I added it to my long list. I looked at all the upcoming bills and readjusted the budget. I started shopping at Aldi every Wednesday night after studying the weekly specials.

I rocked him in my arms while he had a meltdown. I cooked his meals. I took care of the housework. I went to work. I helped draft his resume. I put feelers out. I found him a job. I reassured him of his worth. When I made him feel better, I felt useful. Apparently, that was my purpose. Yet the scales never tipped back in my direction.

I could never depend on him. Whenever I needed emotional support, something more important trumped my needs. Ironic, too, that despite his I-go-to-the-gym chest and arms, I was the broad shoulders of our relationship. I was more like a mother than a partner, constantly picking up the pieces of the fallen Jenga tower and rearranging them back into a neat block.

I had never imagined being the kind of woman who would accept this kind of relationship, yet here I was with another needy man. It was complex because of the payoffs we were both receiving. I felt worthy and Adrian felt safe. For a long time, I was oblivious to how mentally detrimental the enmeshment was for us both. But over time, I began to acknowledge my part in the relationship. I realised I couldn't keep blaming Adrian for what I was putting up with.

A year later, Adrian was more settled in his new job, but nothing had changed for me. I was sick of putting up with the mediocrity of who we were as a couple. I arrived home from work one day with an idea. I didn't understand it then, but I must have been testing him. At the time, we were renting a unit not far from where I worked.

'There's a brand-new place I've seen that I think would be a good buy instead of wasting all this money on rent,' I said.

'Where's this come from all of a sudden?'

'Well, I've had the money from my other place sitting in the bank for a few years now, and I think it's a good time to buy. Nothing has really caught my eye until now, but I've got a really good feeling about this one. You know how my gut just knows.'

I was beginning to appreciate the strength of these subtle messages. For once, I wanted to follow the divine guidance I had so often ignored.

'Can we even afford to buy a place?' Adrian clenched his teeth.

It was the complete opposite to what I desperately needed him to say: *Sure, baby, let's look into this. We can work this out together.*

Yeah, right. I must have been dreaming. I had desperately wanted him to step up, but looking back, I wonder whether I was secretly willing him to fail my test. I was thinking, *If he can't give me some kind of certainty, how can I rely on him in the future and how on earth are we ever going to be able to start a family without my income?*

'It will be just like paying rent. We can always sell if we need to. The market is probably the lowest it can go. Can you at least think about it?' I pleaded.

Adrian paced around the room, blank-faced, unsettled.

We contemplated for too long. There were seven units in the complex, and they all sold quickly. I placed a photo of the property on the divider wall above my computer at work, a 'Clayton's' vision board, activating my ability to manifest things. If we were meant to buy it, we would. One of the sales fell over a few weeks later, and we were back in discussions.

'But what if anything happens between us?' Adrian asked. 'It's all your money, and I don't want to be thrown out on the street. If we break up, you'd say it's your place and make me leave.'

'As if I'd do that,' I said. 'Would it make you feel better if we had a solicitor draw something up?'

He agreed and to my surprise, he passed my test, albeit a little reluctantly. I see only now that we were planning for our demise before we signed the contract.

In my previous relationship with Scott, I had occupied the same role. I booked the restaurants and holidays. I shopped. I decided what we would eat. I was the driver. I didn't drink. How could I, when I was the responsible one that needed to get us home safe? He couldn't handle his alcohol, so I always refrained from drinking at parties and events. I sacrificed having fun because I didn't feel safe.

'Has he got his jumper?' Scott's mum asked one night before we went to the football.

'Don't worry. I've got it.'

'I'm glad you're here, darl. My job is done, and you can take over looking after him.'

I didn't have any children but had the job of being the sensible one, holding up the net for the men in my life to fall into.

'Make sure you look after yourself and don't rely on anyone else,' Dad had always told me.

Him and Mum had been through financial troubles back in the eighties when interest rates rose to nearly eighteen percent.

Only in my thirties did I realise how much impact that one simple sentence had had on me. To uphold his advice, I had been acting as if I didn't need anyone, but what my heart wanted more than anything *was* to share life's responsibilities with someone. I didn't want to always have to be the powerful one because my partners failed to step up.

But the partners I kept choosing were never going to fulfil my needs. They were incapable of standing up or meeting my desires. Maybe I had chosen them for that exact reason. *Ouch*. Perhaps I was unknowingly encouraging it to happen, demanding what my heart never truly wanted. It could never end well.

All I knew was that I was tired of being the mother to the men in my life. Everything in its place made Mum happy. But I was not my mother. Having men in their place did not make me happy.

The pattern I had been trapped in all my life was about to be broken.

7

STOLEN GRIEF

I stood in the shower holding a hard-bristled brush that kept falling to the side as I'd scrubbed the walls. My knuckles were swollen and bright pink. I hadn't noticed my fingers rubbing against the tiles. My face was close to the wall where I could concentrate on brushing every grain of sand in the grout. The intensity made me breathless. I kept swapping arms. It didn't matter that the shower was already clean.

Ten minutes earlier, Mum had called from three hundred kilometres away.

'They found a spot on Dad's lung.'

'They got it wrong last week. They could have it wrong again.'

'Not this time. They have done all the tests. It's,' Mum took a deep breath, 'mesothelioma.'

'What?'

'From asbestos.'

'What can they do for that?'

As she spoke, I began to imagine people with tubes from their noses.

'They're finding out more every day. His doctor is the top surgeon in Sydney. He's even been on TV. On RPA.' Mum was babbling on, scrambling for the positive. I couldn't care that my dad's health was in the hands of a TV celebrity. But if he really was the best, I had to have faith that this miracle doctor could fix him.

There was zero emotion in my tone as I relayed the news to Adrian. 'It's lung cancer…Dad.'

He returned a blank, useless look. I picked up the shower cleaner and brush from the laundry cupboard. I shut the ensuite door. I needed a barrier between us.

As with BC and AD, a line had been drawn, forever dividing my life into before the news and after it. My urge to know more was swift, strong. I needed to find out everything I could about a disease that hadn't been the slightest bit important to me one day earlier – when it wasn't my problem or my dad's.

Over the years, I'd found lumps in my breasts, had strange sensations here and sharp pains there, but the tests had always revealed nothing serious. Waiting for results always gave me a tight stomach, until *phew*, I could exhale when the results showed it was a false alarm and everything could go back to normal. Now I waited for the same relief. But this was different. Dad could never go back to the life he knew. Neither could I.

I stood under the showerhead and let the water envelop me,

hearing nothing but the flow. I clenched my teeth. My mind turned to Adrian. *Why was I still with him?* I knew he wasn't the man for me. I had known for a while, but there I was, still gearing up for the 'right time' to tell him it was over, trying to protect his feelings. I was making the same mistake I'd made twice before. I needed to stop procrastinating, but it was all too much. Getting out of the relationship felt urgent, but could I cope with another break-up on top of Dad's sickness? I knew I was delaying the inevitable, but I was also emotionally spent.

The first funeral I'd ever attended had been only a couple of years earlier for my dad's mate, Neville. I had a strong feeling as I was sitting there watching his daughter deliver the eulogy, that I would have to do the same someday soon. Then my Nanna died six months after Neville, disrupting the comfort I'd always had that the flourishing branches of my family tree – a majestic white oak – were protecting me from above.

I had so little experience of death and suddenly, it was all around me. I'd always thought I could take my time. I imagined I had a lifetime ahead of me. What was the rush?

After I got off the phone from Mum, a thought accosted me. *If Dad dies, what will I say at his funeral?*

That's when I started to scrub the walls of the shower.

'I could be dead tomorrow,' Dad always used to joke. It was his justification for enjoying the simple pleasures in life, said with a clack of the tongue, a cheeky wink and a sideways flick of his head. The phrase slid from his mouth like butter over a freshly baked cinnamon teacake. He'd offer it up while laughing with the neighbours when he was supposed to be mowing the lawn. With his famous 'shoot the bastards' and 'bloody' this or 'bloody' that comments, he would crack open a home-brewed beer or a *Tooheys New* after a hard day's work or following a round of golf on a Saturday afternoon.

He called our family friend 'Bloody Vicki,' which made her giggle – she knew it was a sign of endearment. He referred to me, Mum and Kim as 'my girls' and he'd shout 'Jesus Christ' in place of the 'F' word to express his frustrations. His language, although oftentimes not politically correct, uniquely identified him. His voice, kind but loud, with an unmistakable Aussie twang, made people feel instantly welcome.

It took Dad to get sick for me to realise *I* could be dead tomorrow.

* * *

Dad didn't die on 19 May 2011. His death certificate lied. Google killed him fourteen months earlier.

A couple of days after Mum's phone call, I typed *mesothelioma* in the long thin box on the computer at work. As I scrolled down, it flashed in front of my eyes. That one *bloody* paragraph changed my life forever. There was no cure and ninety-five percent of patients do not survive two years after diagnosis. *Why did I look?* I hope Google slept that night. I didn't.

As I sat at my desk that day, I held my ladybird pendant between my finger and thumb. It usually comforted me. Adrian had given it to me early on in our relationship for good luck. Now I just wanted to rip it from my neck.

All my life, I'd feared just this: my parents dying. I needed them. They had guided me through every life decision. The thought of either of them not being here was incomprehensible. I'd always said I was the luckiest girl alive to have such a wonderful family, the best mother and father anyone could ask for. My love for them was wide and deep. Now my worst fear was real.

Rachael must have heard me pulling tissues from the box. She popped her head around the barrier that divided our desks. I didn't speak. I pointed to the computer screen.

'Oh, honey.'

'What am I going to do?'

'There's nothing you can do,' she said as she hugged me.

I started grieving that day for the father I was about to lose. And I grieved too for the decades of my own life that I'd already lost.

After Dad's diagnosis in March 2010, bad news became contagious. Six months later, my Pop, Dad's father, died after suffering with dementia for several years. Nanna, Dad's mother, held on for twenty-six days only before she too passed away after a routine knee operation. She couldn't recover after her soulmate left her.

As a wide-eyed little girl, I remember sitting on Nanna's knee on the dressing table chair, as she told me how they'd met out the back of the ambulance station where she lived. I'd play with her oval locket necklace with my tiny fingers, scratched and faded from biannual caravan trips to Avoca Beach over the years. It contained worn sepia-toned photos of Nanna and Pop as teenagers. She was a classic beauty, and he was debonair. They looked like movie stars. They were fourteen when they met, eighty-seven when they died – a seventy-three-year love story.

In her last days, she choked on her words, her voice

unrecognisable. 'I wanna go with Reg. Please let me go.'

I'd held her purple and bruised hand. Her skin was so thin, not the hands with which she once baked custard tarts and played tennis.

'I don't want to do this anymore. Let me be with Reg.'

Her pleas were the desperate wail of a woman expelling her anguish. Nanna had always been strong, but she died of a broken heart. I also believe she didn't want to witness her own son die.

We weren't to know at the time, but Dad only lasted another eight months. And while Dad was dying, he had to grieve the loss of both of his parents.

The ancestral foliage I'd taken for granted no longer shielded me.

I began to associate the ringtone on my phone with this terrible time in my life. So much so, I had to change it.

Mum's dad – my last remaining grandparent – died the following year. So many people I loved were dying, and it was all happening way too fast.

You have my attention now, I said to Whoever Was In Charge.

During this time, Adrian needed a lot of consoling. He couldn't cope with what was happening with my dad. I needed him more than I ever had, but he couldn't offer me anything.

'This is as hard for me as it is for you, you know,' he once told me.

'Really?' was all I managed in response.

Adrian moped around for the entire year leading up to Dad's death. At the mention of Dad's name, he'd wilt, saying, 'It's all too much for me.'

One day a neighbour commented, 'I've never seen anyone make it so much about them when their partner's parent is dying.'

Adrian kept trying to steal my grief.

His mum once called me as I was driving home from work one night to discuss her concerns about her son.

'I'm really worried about Adrian, darl.'

All my loss rose up inside me. And that's when I snapped.

'I'm really worried too. I'm worried that he can't cope when I'm not there to pick up the pieces. He is crumbling. He doesn't know what to do. Do you know why he doesn't know what to do? Because every single day for the last four years, I've reassured him, pepped him up and boosted his confidence. And right now, my dad is close to dying, his parents have just died… and I…I haven't got *anything* else to give. Nothing. I'm empty. So, yes, I am concerned about him too. But I'm afraid for the first time, he's not my priority right now.'

Had I just said that out loud?

I hadn't paused during the entire rant. But I'd reached my limit.

She stuttered, stunned and agreed she'd speak to Adrian.

When Nanna and Pop passed away, they left a few thousand dollars for all four of their grandchildren. It couldn't have come at a better time for me, and I am forever grateful for their generosity. With Dad so ill, and Adrian not coping, I decided to use that money to get away on my own to The Golden Door Health Retreat in the Hinterland in Queensland.

It was the perfect place to visit solo and one I'd dreamed about before I even knew it existed. Back at uni, one of our major assignments for Tourism Marketing was to prepare a full business plan with diagrams, budgets and ideas for how to promote a business of my choice. I concocted a place where the entry foyer was a hexagonal shape; and leading from each of the six sides was a day spa, gym, book shop and library, room for meditation and yoga, private and luxurious accommodation, and a restaurant that served healthy food. I was only twenty years old and didn't know that places like this actually existed. I loved inventing this wonderful, make-believe place.

Years later, when I was working as a sales executive in the Sydney head office of Cypress Lakes Resort, they purchased The Golden Door Health Retreat in Queensland. I visited twice, once in 2004 and again in 2005.

Now with this gift from my nanna and pop many years later, I booked my third visit and spent hours flipping through the retreat booklet, choosing treatments and wellness appointments.

This time I might find myself, I hoped. *I mustn't have looked hard enough previously.*

Of all the options on offer, I chose a counselling session – I hadn't ever tried it before. *Finally, someone experienced and with a proper qualification would be able to tell me exactly what to do about Adrian.*

8

GUILTY WHEN INNOCENT

'Are you guys headed for the health retreat?' a man asked. I noticed what a kind face he had.

'We are,' I replied.

He extended his hand to shake mine and a woman, Jen, I'd just met at the airport. He introduced himself as Mark.

'Nice to meet you both.'

He sounded like an Aussie ocker version of Sean Connery.

Mark told us he'd been to The Golden Door in the Hunter Valley a few times. 'They convinced me to come to this one, so it's my first time here.'

'Are you escaping too, Mark? Seems like a common theme,' Jen smiled.

'I actually bought a voucher for myself and my wife for

Christmas,' he said. 'But she wasn't very impressed. Said it was always about me, so here I am, with a spare ticket for another time. It was the straw that broke the camel's back, I suppose.' He paused for a couple of seconds before saying, 'We've separated.'

Jen and I glanced at each other.

'If someone gave me a week at a health retreat, it would be the best gift ever. My father is really sick, and I needed to take some time out for a bit,' I told him.

'Oh, I'm sorry,' Mark said before one of the staff members called for our attention.

'Hi, I'm Pete. Welcome to Brisbane, everyone. Are you ready to be transformed?'

A burbled yes from the group.

'I said, *are you ready?*'

'Yes,' the group shouted in unison with a few awkward giggles.

'It's going to be a great week. The buses are here, so if you could put your bags in the back and hop on board, we'll head for the property and get you settled in. If you want anything to eat, grab something now as you won't be eating for a week… just kidding, ha ha ha.'

There were a few blank looks, but we all soon caught on to Pete's sense of humour.

Mark, Jen and I always sat together at mealtimes. It's funny how in situations with strangers, we gravitate to the ones we meet first. I loved that no-one talked about work. There was no 'What do you do?' talk. All we knew about each other were our common interests. Conversation was mainly about how we were each trying to live a healthier lifestyle and reduce our stress.

Most mornings, Mark and I walked together during the bush walks, speaking nonstop.

'I'm reading a book called *The Power* at the moment. It's the follow on to *The Secret*. Something positive after so much negativity.'

'Sounds good,' Mark replied. 'I listen to Tony Robbins a lot and other life coaches like Stephen Covey.'

'I love Tony Robbins. I've been to his live event. It was life changing. I've read a few of his books too.'

'Oh, I've always wanted to go to see him,' Mark said.

I was attracted to Mark then and there, and secretly wished Adrian and I had already broken up. But I wasn't going to do the wrong thing by Adrian even if I knew we were over. I made do with our connection, which felt nourishing and wholesome.

On the fourth day, my counselling session was coming up and I was feeling a little anxious.

'I've never been to a counsellor before,' I said to Mark. 'I just want to confirm the inevitable about my relationship with Adrian.'

Oh. The words seeped out like an oil spill.

Mark just nodded but said nothing.

Why do I always give so much information? My name would surely pop up beside verbal diarrhoea in the dictionary.

Bronwyn, the counsellor in her mid-forties, sat composed behind the desk; and I sat on the caramel-coloured lounge. A burning sensation spread across my cheeks and down my neck. I had no idea what to expect.

I waited for her to break the silence.

'So, Lisa, tell me a little bit about yourself.'

I told her about my grandparents and how Dad was terminally ill. I paused for, oh, two seconds before adding, as if it was superfluous information, 'And I'm not very happy in my relationship. I would have actually left him earlier, but with all this going on, there's been too much to deal with all at once.'

I knew that everything else was out of my control, but I had the power to change my relationship.

'I always seem to be pepping him up and constantly having to reassure him.'

'Do you realise that's the third time you've said that?' she said as she jotted something down on her notepaper.

I uncrossed and re-crossed my legs. My red face became redder. Bronwyn did a lot of nodding and didn't say much. I wasn't expecting that. Where were her brilliant insights and confirmation that I had no choice but to leave Adrian? The allocated time seemed to pass rapidly, and her advice in the end was anticlimactic.

'What you need to do is live the next three months as if there are no problems, and if things don't change after that, you know what to do.'

I felt robbed. Like I'd wasted my wellness consultation. *Where was the signed declaration that there was no future in our relationship?* I needed something I could hand to Adrian. To prove to him that a professional agreed with me and saw no hope for us. I couldn't trust my own feelings. I doubted my own certainty. My grief had made me delusional. My conditioning had made me avoidant. I couldn't bear to even think about giving us another three months. *And then another three, then another three,* a small voice inside whispered. I wanted an easy way out.

Why do I keep making the same mistakes?

Over the remaining days at The Golden Door, I promised myself I would not make this same mistake again. I didn't want the week to end. I loved having a cabin to myself. For the first time in years, I didn't feel suffocated. I read motivational books. There were no televisions, and I wasn't exposed to any external stimuli. I also became more grounded each day after Tai Chi, stretch class, a treatment at the spa and loads of physical exercise. Delicious healthy food and early nights fuelled my body with the nutrients and rest it needed to heal and recuperate. It was a detox for my body and my mind. On the last day, I felt like a new woman.

When it ended, most people headed for Sydney or Melbourne. Mark and I were the only guests travelling to Newcastle Airport from Brisbane. As I approached the carousel, the smile I'd worn at the health retreat all week faded. It wasn't going to follow me out the doors of the airport. *Maybe someone would put it in the lost and found so I could pick it up later.*

Then I spotted him – the cap, singlet, over-trained upper body. It was hard to miss. After a quick kiss and a hug, Adrian's loving 'welcome home' expression disappeared.

'Adrian, this is Mark. Mark, Adrian. Mark was at The Golden Door too.'

Silence erupted. Adrian interlaced his fingers as his stance became awkward and standoffish. His chest expanded like an over-baked cake about to split. I waited for smoke to waft out of his every pore.

'Nice to meet you,' Mark said.

Adrian grumbled, 'Hi,' in response.

Mark waved goodbye, sensing the tension. I'd told him how possessive Adrian was. I felt deflated thinking I'd likely never see Mark again.

Adrian took my bag and headed to the car in absolute silence.

'Are you really going to do this to me?' I didn't recognise my own high-pitched voice at first. 'I can't believe after the amazing week I've had, you're doing this.'

'Doing what? Hmph. So…is he single? Did you have dinner with him?' His voice thundered.

In an instant, I was back on alert, scrambling for an answer to appease him, to stop him from getting angry in the hope of attracting the lesser punishment. If he'd known I had spent the week with other men, he would have been insane with jealousy. I could see it on his face – the regret that he'd 'let' me go beyond his control.

'He actually recently split up with his wife, and yes, sometimes I sat with him. The whole group all sat together at big round tables. There were only five tables. As if he would have been interested in me anyway.'

I took deep breaths to hold back the tears that rippled upwards from my stomach to my throat. My usual state of panic returned like muscle memory.

He wrapped his hands around the steering wheel, his knuckles white. I didn't want to look at him, but out of the corner of my eye, I saw him shake his head the way a disappointed parent does to a child.

'And here I was at home missing you, and *you're* off having a great old time with *him*. He looks like a skinny nerd anyway.'

'You always have to turn everything around. I can't believe you're even saying this. Nothing happened. He's just a friend. I'll probably never see him again anyway. Why do you always have to put everyone down?'

'I'm sure you've organised to keep in touch.'

'We haven't, actually, but there's no point in telling you because you never believe a word I say. You really don't trust me, do you?'

He screeched the tyres of his precious car, sub-woofer blaring.

I closed my eyes, took a deep breath and kicked myself for having introduced them. I had nothing to hide. But I should have known to shut up.

My cheeks felt tight and sticky where the trail of tears had dried up during the silent hour's drive home. There was no point in talking. All I ever seemed to do was explain myself. I'd gone to get away from all the stress and drama. Now my face was puffy again, and any mending that had been done was unravelled. I wanted to scream so loud that people in their cars could hear and would pull over to come help me. All I wanted to do was go back to that special place, away from Adrian. But that would have been escaping from my life, delaying the inevitable. And we weren't even home yet.

The truth is, I was thinking about Mark as I stared out the window. Probably more so because Adrian had made such a big deal of him. While we should have been talking about all the great things I'd done and learnt during the week, or catching up on what he'd been up to, instead, I had to defend myself for doing nothing wrong. Again. Guilty of being innocent.

But I was secretly glad I'd met Mark. He had been a sign of hope when all else seemed hopeless. He was confirmation that considerate and interesting men actually existed. I saw him as a sign that when I got through this mess, maybe there would be someone lovely out there for me.

9

WASTED TIME

I could taste the salt in the back of my throat. I couldn't stop the tears as I drove home from my parents' home near Port Macquarie. I probably shouldn't have been driving, especially not on my own. My hands gripped the steering wheel so hard there were two thick red lines embedded in my palms. My jaw ached.

I was going to break up with Adrian. Until then, I had always come up with excuses, but everything was different now. I no longer had a dad. A couple of weeks ago, I had made a promise to my dying father, and I'd never felt motivation like this before.

The noise of the V8's motor compounded the adrenaline pumping through my body. The car had been Adrian's choice

– an attention-seeking machine. It was fire-engine red for a start. As I drove the three-hour trip on the lonely road home, I screamed the lyrics of Gloria Estefan's 'Always Tomorrow' through my tears. What a sight I must have been to any passing cars – a girl with a patchy red face belting out tunes as if she were on stage. Can you believe I still self-identified as a 'girl' even though I was a thirty-six-year-old woman? As I sang, I thought of all I'd survived in the past year – it had been the hardest time of my life.

The day before we lost Dad, I'd told him my secret while he lay in his hospital bed, exhaling in pain. They were trialling a new mesothelioma medication on him. Instead of helping, it sped up his demise. I'm still conflicted as to whether I should have been angry about that or thankful.

'My toes.' He grimaced, baring his ever-so-familiar teeth. 'They're so sore.'

Kim and I could spot Dad easily in a crowd because the bottom right corner of his front tooth was missing. It ruined his disguise one year when he dressed up as Santa at the tennis Christmas party. That and his familiar watch, his thick gold wedding ring and contagious laugh. He'd chipped his tooth with the back of a hammer before I was born and had never fixed it.

'Do you want me to rub them?' I asked, not knowing what else to do.

He tilted his head and the corners of his mouth. I interpreted the gesture as, 'It can't hurt,' but it did.

I studied his toes as I rubbed them gently. They were icy-cold, blacky-purple. They looked bruised. *Had he kicked his foot?* I didn't know then that gangrene had set in. His body had started to die before he did.

A long, low sound came from deep within him. 'It's excruciating,' he'd groaned.

I'd covered his feet with the sheet and sat back down in the ugly blue faux leather chair at the foot of the bed. I knew it well. I'd clocked up over three thousand kilometres driving back and forth those last few weeks. I wanted to sit there with him and Mum, who hadn't moved from the right corner of the room, arms and legs crossed. Her hair was perfectly flicked and styled. Even in this moment, it would have been odd to see her with a hair out of place. She kept commenting that the air-conditioning was 'bloody freezing.' After being with Dad for four decades, she'd adopted some of his quirky language.

We sat in silence and watched him as he lay there, waiting for the pain to stop. Waiting. Everyone responded differently to their grief. Kim stayed away. She didn't want to see him like this. I didn't blame her. She wanted to hold on to happy memories.

Every so often, Dad would struggle to and from the toilet, and I'd strangle my threatening tears. His stomach protruded like that of starving Ethiopian children on the World Vision ads. In these moments, I avoided Mum's gaze. She held her emotions inside like she had always done and as she'd modelled for us.

This isn't my dad, I thought as I looked at him, still in total disbelief. Mum and I were skinny and tired, but every now and then, we'd get the energy for some chit-chat while Dad was drifting in and out of sleep.

One day Mum asked what Adrian had been doing. I raised my left eyebrow. 'Don't worry. He won't be here for much longer.'

In that moment, Dad's eyes sprang open; he was clearly lucid. Earlier, they'd been rolling between his half-open eyelids, which made him look all groggy and distant. *Had he thought I was talking about him?*

'I mean Adrian, Dad. He won't be around for much longer. I'm going to sort everything out when I go home.'

I had been to-ing and fro-ing about whether to tell Dad or not. But now it seemed I'd decided to.

'It's about time,' Mum said.

'I know I should have done it sooner. But when I get back, I'm going to get my life sorted. I'm not wasting any more time.'

I didn't need to say anything else.

Adrian admired Dad. He looked up to him and regarded him as a father figure. He would have been devastated to know that in the last few months when they'd gone fishing, Dad had pretended to be ill so he could go home. He couldn't stand how competitive Adrian was. He only had a few months to live and wanted to skip conversations about who was 'the best fisherman' and who'd 'caught the most.'

After Dad's funeral, Adrian got a lift home with his parents while I had stayed the week with Mum. As I neared home, I was almost out of tears, a mixture of sadness from losing Dad and anxiety about the upheaval ahead. During Dad's demise and death, I'd been distracted. Now I had to confront the reality of my own life and face the hard stuff. It was going to hurt. But I could no longer live an inauthentic life. There was no time to waste.

All Dad had ever wanted was for his daughters to be happy. Maybe I'd needed the ultimate accountability from someone I could never discuss this with again.

At his hospital bed, I'd spoken my final word on the subject, and I knew I had to uphold it. Dad would be watching and checking I'd made good on my promise. Dad had always been protective of Mum. He'd adored her and was always joking around and teasing her. He'd grab her on the bum as he walked past or give her a cheeky wink and a laugh.

I had none of this in my relationship. Adrian was serious. Insecure. Paranoid.

When I pulled into the garage, I put my hand on my stomach and took some deep breaths. I'd never been so fatigued, yet I had renewed strength. As I carried my bags up the stairs, I could still see Dad's eyes when I said those words and how the corner of his lips moved. His face told me he'd heard and that he approved.

Nothing was going to stop me keeping my word to the only man I'd ever truly relied on.

10

PUZZLING ALLERGIES

While I was with Adrian, I often developed red rashes on my arms and face. I also got cramps after every meal and had chronic diarrhoea and bloating. Was I allergic to something I was eating? This had been going on for so long I considered it normal. It was a running joke at work that I used most of the toilet paper.

'We'll have to deduct some money from your pay.'

After I returned from The Golden Door, I consulted with a nutritionist, Ryan, who suggested some tests, including a colonoscopy.

But everything was normal.

Ryan scratched his forehead as he studied the detailed pages of my food diary, which showed pretty close to perfect, clean eating.

'This doesn't make sense. What else is going on in your life?'

'Well, I haven't been happy in my relationship for a while.'

I jumped as he slammed my food diary shut. He tilted his head. His voice was calm, matter-of-fact. 'If you're not happy, you'd better get the hell out…and fast. Your body is rebelling.'

It wasn't the diagnosis I was expecting.

It turns out I wasn't allergic to any particular food, rather I couldn't tolerate not being true to myself.

It would have been easier to get a medical diagnosis so I could pass the responsibility for my health to a doctor. Now the burden was mine. *Shit.* My health was being affected. You'd think this would make it easy for me to take action. But still I struggled. I had been through so much grief and just wanted to catch my breath. I needed to regather my strength for the imminent emotional turmoil. I waited a couple of months and then took a half-step.

At home alone one Saturday morning, I prepared myself to initiate the conversation I needed to have with Adrian by drawing an invisible energy towards my heart with my cupped hands. *You can do it. Deep breaths.*

When Adrian walked in, I just came out with it.

'I've had some time to think today and I…I just want you to know that I'm going to sleep in the spare room.'

He looked away for a second, then turned back with a peculiar expression on his face.

'I'm not coping, and I need to sort a few things out.'

'It's because of your dad, isn't it?'

'It's what I want.'

'It's just because you're upset. It will be fine.'

'I haven't been happy for a while. What's happened to Dad has made me realise how short life is.'

In my mind, 'we' were already over, and I didn't want to sleep in the same bed, in 'our' room. I was in the torturous in-between place – physically still there but emotionally not. Every part of my being was long gone. I had been preparing my departure for many months – years, in fact. But I had to remember that for Adrian, this was breaking news.

Earlier in our relationship, when I was still trying, I had attempted to get Adrian to watch the movie *The Secret*. I'd read the book by Rhonda Byrne and from it had learned about the law of attraction – that we attract what we focus on. What did I hope he'd get out of it? That he would find himself? Feel less paranoid? Maybe simply that we'd find some common ground in our interests.

In the bedroom, I'd switched the TV on and started playing it, hoping it would hook him. After a few minutes he'd shot out a quick breath.

'I can't watch this crap.'

'You haven't even given it a chance.'

'I think I've seen enough.' He'd stormed out to the lounge room to watch *Alien vs. Predator*.

'Can you at least turn it down?' I'd yelled as I marched down the hallway, slamming the bedroom door behind me.

Every night while I was sleeping in the spare room, Adrian would knock on the door and open it before I answered. My body would stiffen as soon as he entered.

'C'mon. This is silly. Please come back. I want you in our bed.'

'I'm staying here. Please don't do this to me.'

'Do *what?* Just come back. I can't sleep without you beside me. C'mon.'

I'd glare at him.

I didn't tell him that I couldn't sleep *with* him beside me. I didn't tell him that my stomach cramped when he was around, that his endless questions made me feel ill. I didn't tell him I was tired of being pressured into spending every second with him when I wasn't at work. I didn't tell him I'd had enough of him acting as though he was superior and smarter than me. I didn't tell him I couldn't bear the way I was interrogated on the rare occasions I was 'let out' to see my friends. I didn't tell him I was sick of having to describe the age, height and weight of any male tradesperson who visited our home. I didn't tell him I was infuriated by his mood changes and the way he instigated arguments seemingly for no reason. I still didn't speak up.

He'd sit on the end of the bed looking at me with sad puppy eyes.

'Please.'

'For goodness' sake, can't you just let me be?' On one such night, just to get him to leave me alone, I flung the covers off and stomped back into the main bedroom. 'Are you happy now?'

In those moments, I had never felt so alone lying beside someone I didn't want to be with. How deluded was he to think that my coming back into the room, lying on my back without touching him, breathing heavy cranky breaths, would make him feel better? Why couldn't I just make a clean break? During those bleak hours, I realised that Adrian, as selfish, manipulative and controlling as he was, did not deserve this.

At work the next morning, I greeted my friend Michelle with a wave but didn't speak.

She reversed back into the office.

'What's wrong?'

'Nothing,' I said sheepishly.

'You went back, didn't you?'

'Just for one night. I was too tired to fight. He was so persistent.'

She put her hand up in the air – a stop sign.

'I don't want to talk to you. Do you realise how far this has set you back? I'm *so* disappointed,' she said, her voice fading as she retreated. But I heard every word, and I have never forgotten that moment.

No-one was more disappointed than me. What was becoming clear was that my inability to act had begun to affect my friendships. I was losing the respect of people who were trying to support me.

American entrepreneur, author and business strategist, Tony Robbins, teaches techniques to help us get out of predicaments. He asks you to project five years into the future and imagine what your life will be like if you don't make any changes. *Would you be sick? Would you still have the support of your family...your friends?* I knew that what I was doing – or not doing – was infuriating for my loved ones. I also knew that they wouldn't put up with my weakness forever. Friends and family are supportive to a point but become frustrated when we don't seem to want to be helped.

As I was trying to move forward with my life, Adrian kept

trying desperately to pull me back in a last-ditch effort to save the relationship. One afternoon he practically dragged me into a jewellery shop. He had no idea I'd already been speaking to a solicitor.

'No. Let's not do this now,' I said, walking the other way.

'Why not? I just want to see what you like and what suits you.'

I didn't want a ring. I wanted to be on my own and find out who I was without the distraction of a helpless man. I had to make it blatantly clear. I could not prolong this anymore. When we got home, I told him we needed to speak.

'I can't keep going on like this. I haven't been happy for a while now, and I don't want to hurt you, but this is not working. I want to be on my own.'

'You're breaking up?'

'I'm sorry. All we do is fight, and I don't ever seem to make you happy. *I'm* not happy.'

I pulled out paperwork from the folder I had brought to the table.

'What's this?'

'I've spoken to a solicitor.'

'Great. So there's *no* chance?'

'I've thought very deeply about what I want, and I can't go on anymore without complete honesty. It's not fair on either of us.'

'Can't we just wait and give it another go?

'It's too late for that.'

I hated the confused, angry-but-sad look on his face.

I'd worked out a fair and equal way that I could keep the

unit, given what we'd each paid so far. I'd paid the deposit and all the original costs. Adrian would get the car that was almost fully paid and other assets, and we'd split the savings. There'd been a sale of the identical unit next door in recent weeks, so we had a direct comparable sale to determine the market value at the time.

Mum had offered to help me out by loaning me some money for a few months while I made arrangements to refinance and service the loan on my own, but Adrian would have to agree. My heart raced as I showed him the breakdown.

'I can't cope with moving and finding another place after all that I'd been through.' The relief of simply voicing it and getting it out of my body made me burst into tears.

'I need to get a solicitor to look at this,' he said with flared nostrils.

'Of course. That would be the smart thing to do,' I sniffed.

'I'm not paying though. You can. I don't want this.'

'Okay, I'll pay.'

And just like that. It was done – three months after my promise to Dad.

The break-up became real. It was no longer a phase I was going through. The roller coaster was finally about to stop. Adrian believed my change of heart was because I wasn't coping with Dad's death. But it was the opposite. There was no point trying to explain that his controlling behaviour was making me physically sick. I didn't want to hear any more justifications or get embroiled in any more arguments. I had to run fast from this relationship. I had to make good on my promise to dad.

* * *

'You certainly are holding onto a lot of *stuff*, Lisa,' Jodie, my massage therapist, said as she worked her magic on my back. I'd told her about my dad and Adrian as I sniffed through the hole in the table.

It was impossible to hold the tears in. The kneading drew the emotion and stress from my body. I felt everything go limp. I didn't have to be strong for anyone else. I didn't have to hold my body taut and on guard. Every muscle relaxed.

'You should write a list,' Jodie said.

'A list?'

'Yeah, a list. Of everything you want in a partner.'

'You mean…like a tick list?'

I believed in the law of attraction, yet it felt superficial to write this kind of list. *Isn't that kind of thing supposed to happen naturally, not by submitting an order?*

'Trust me. When you're ready, write a list. Just put down the qualities that you would love in the man of your dreams.'

A few weeks later, I wrote my list. Just for fun.

1) Makes me laugh.
2) Trusts me.
3) Makes me feel safe.
4) Adventurous.
5) Allows me to be myself.

When I finished, I'd listed over thirty qualities. I folded my list in half and put it in my pack of Titania's Fortune Cards and forgot about it.

* * *

Once we'd agreed on all the financial decisions, Adrian and I lived as flat mates. We'd officially broken up, but the deed of agreement we'd signed stated we could both live in the unit until it was sold. And that's exactly what he did. To the day. Even though he was moving back in with his parents and could have left sooner, he stayed another few weeks. He only moved out on the day his name was taken off the title and I owned the unit outright.

As soon as the door closed behind him, my terrible cramps disappeared. My skin cleared up. The tension in my jaw left.

But best of all, I'd honoured my promise to my father. And my heart felt light for the first time in years.

PART TWO
Giving Up

11

SPIRITUAL RECIPE

Soon after I returned to work after Dad died, I followed Rachael's suggestion and joined a local meditation group.

At the first meeting, friendly faces comforted me as I sat cross-legged on the floor at Christopher and Amy's home.

Christopher's voice was as mesmerising as the open fire. I closed my eyes and instantly was thrust into the darkness I had come to escape.

Thick air strangled my throat. I felt as if I was suffocating. 'Ahem…ahem.'

I was conscious of being the one who kept interrupting the peaceful silence. *I'm usually good at this,* I thought. *What was wrong with me?*

Inside me, everything was loud. *Boom. Boom. Boom.*

I took quick, desperate 'survival' breaths. I loosened the scarf from my neck, but I was having a full-blown panic attack under the most unexpected circumstances. The room was spinning. I couldn't focus on my breath. It was too confronting. I was conscious of my exaggerated swallowing and the constant need to clear my throat, which surely would have distracted the others.

Please, let this end soon. I felt as if I was close to passing out.

After half an hour – which seemed like eternity – I heard, 'Okay, slowly start to bring some movement back into your body. Take your time, and when you are ready, slowly open your eyes.'

I was breathing again. *I was still alive.*

'I'm so sorry,' I said later as we congregated in the kitchen for homemade masala chai from a big silver pot. 'I'm not usually like this. It's just that my dad passed away five weeks ago.'

'There's no need to apologise. You're exactly where you need to be,' Christopher said.

And I was – for the first time in a long time. Here, I had a chance to slow down; and in doing so, I could begin to grieve Dad, feel all the loss and start healing. While I was in survival mode, I had numbed everything, but I had to give myself time to focus on what I'd been through and what it meant for the remainder of my life. I was sick of 'doing.' It was time to learn how to 'be.'

Over the coming months, I began to enjoy the meditations.

One night when I was driving home, a streetlight turned off at the exact moment I was under it. It felt a bit spooky, and I wondered if it was just a coincidence. But the following week, at our meditation session, Christopher mentioned that people who have passed often communicate with us through electricity. Later that night, as I drove home with my friend Lauren, I pointed out the light that had gone out the previous week.

'That one,' I said as we approached it.

We were leaning towards the windscreen as we drove under it and let out a joint squeal as the light came back on again. We were both flabbergasted.

'Oh my god,' Lauren said, clutching her chest.

'That was pretty freaky,' I said. But I wasn't freaked out.

I have always been comforted by the feeling that the Universe is looking out for me. I also believe in reincarnation and that we each have a soul group we keep meeting up with in different forms each time we return.

I have no doubt that our souls are all interlinked – this book is a culmination of my story and all the stories of my ancestors before me. They have guided the greater story of where I've come from. I'm just a tiny speck in a greater picture. They had their role and I have mine. I could not have written this without the assistance of my spirit counsellors, particularly, my nanna – Dad's mum. I feel she is always close. I often hear her voice when I'm listening for guidance.

I have sought solace from my spirit guides and have always had a zest to learn more. As a child, I used to read encyclopedias. It didn't matter what I was learning about – anything from the lifecycle of frogs to the history of the Egyptian pharaohs would suffice, my eyes widening when I discovered *anything* I hadn't previously known.

I'm grateful Mum and Dad didn't force religion on us the

way it had been forced on them. They left us to decide for ourselves. Though we were christened and had to learn scripture at school, religion wasn't pushed on us at home.

Nanna prayed before she turned the lights out in Aunty Linda's old room where I always slept when I stayed over. *'Now I lay me down to sleep, I pray the Lord my soul to keep. If I die before I wake, I pray the Lord my soul to take.'*

I'd lie there stiff and frozen, scared to make eye contact with the Jesus statue, my hair tucked under the back of my neck, clutching the sheets and blankets, pulling them up tight under my chin. Eyes wide. Listening to the distracting *tick-tick-tick* of the clock in the dining room until I fell asleep.

As a teenager, I tried to find myself among the endless external white noise of being an adolescent growing up. Although I didn't feel comfortable talking about it with anyone in the family, I was curious about spirituality and all things New Age, as it became popular in the eighties. Kim wasn't interested. Mum and Dad were probably scarred from being forced to go to church when they were growing up. They both stopped attending when they turned eighteen, and it became their own choice.

In my early twenties, I spent most of the money I earned from my part-time job on books, crystals, essential oils, tealight burners and wind chimes. A dozen mobiles or chimes hung from my bedroom ceiling – a collection of suns, moons, fish, cows, teardrops and Japanese symbols. I was comforted by the Native American dreamcatcher above my bed. I had angels literally everywhere around me – figurines, photos, notebooks, pens. Mum would always surprise me with angel-themed gifts too. I was a little obsessed for a while.

I'd spend hours in shops that sold books and spiritual knick-knacks, constantly seeking inspiration.

Some of us return to religion or spirituality when life gets difficult – to seek comfort and support. I have never lost faith. I've always known that there is Someone or Something bigger than me 'out there.' I feel it as a comforting presence. But during the tough years with Adrian, my spirituality deepened.

Losing Dad motivated me even further. I hadn't listened to the gentle hints tapping me on the shoulder. Nothing shook me enough to take drastic action. But someone 'up there' wanted me to look at an alternative route. I imagined them saying, 'We've given her enough time to work it out on her own. She should have received the message by now, but clearly, she hasn't. Let's put something in her face to give her a shove. Things are going to have to get worse before they get better.'

I experience my spirituality as an energetic and vibrational trust of something beyond myself and a connectedness to every other soul. It's not attached to any religion – it's my own recipe. If I don't resonate with certain ingredients, I omit or replace them with others. In this way, I practise an integration of aspects of Christianity, Taoism, Buddhism, Hinduism, as well as the beliefs of many other religions and philosophies. Just like most mothers don't take parenting advice from only one doctor, book or mentor but collect little pieces of wisdom from everywhere and implement what is right for them, I do the same with my spiritual practise.

I honour those who devoutly follow a religion, but it's not for me.

It's been fun creating my own version of faith that serves me. As it turns out, most belief systems have similar intrinsic beliefs at their core: 'treat others as equals,' 'be kind,' 'do unto others,' and 'live in the present moment.' I'm always open to discovering new ideas, and I love learning about the diversity of different cultures.

I've picked up little gems along the way: like the Jewish belief that if you ask for forgiveness from someone three times and they are not willing to grant it, the burden shifts from you to them. I constantly refer to *The Four Agreements* by Don Miguel Ruiz. If I'm ever on a long drive, I listen to the audiobook once again. If everyone lived by the four laws in this book (be impeccable with your word, don't take anything personally, don't make assumptions and always do your best), there would be more love, and less anger and resentment in the world.

I am also drawn to the teachings of the *Tao Te Ching* by the Chinese philosopher Lao Tzu, written in 500BC, the second most-translated book worldwide, surpassed only by the Bible. It teaches us to live in harmony with nature, be authentic, and allow instead of force. It instructs us in detachment and a belief in oneself.

Wayne Dyer's *Change Your Thoughts, Change Your Life* is another cornerstone in my spiritual library. He studied Lao Tzu's eighty-one verses and interprets them so they remain germane in this day and age. Every day I aspire to take a step towards being a Tao-centred person.

I am drawn to spirituality that speaks to our times. Outdated religious beliefs can result in unhealthy sacrifices that don't suit our modern world. The Christian marriage vow, 'Till death do us part,' for example, originated from *The Book of Common Prayer* in the mid-1500s. The original phrase read, 'Till death us depart.' At the time, people lived on average to thirty-five years of age and a marriage would last no longer than twenty years as people got married as young as twelve. To uphold this tradition today, with our much higher life expectancy, might mean sixty or seventy years of marriage. But people and circumstances change over many decades, and it is a different prospect today to stay in abusive or unhappy marriage for half a century because it is against your religion to get a divorce.

What matters to me is how people treat each other – with respect and kindness, no matter the circumstances. We are remembered for the impact we had on others way beyond our time in our physical form.

My relationship to myself and others connects me with God, the Universe, Higher Beings and Spirit. I have never felt the need to prove my faith. It is an inner knowing that defies explanation.

I meditate daily and converse on a higher frequency with my spirit guides and the archangels every single morning. Maybe this is praying. I love spiritual leader and bestselling author Gabrielle Bernstein's view that prayer is when we are asking, and meditation is when we are listening. In meditation, I seek direction, assistance and help to carry out my part of the greater plan for humanity and open myself to the messages I receive.

My guidance often feels like intuition, which is not the same as imagination. As a child, I was taught not to trust those tingly feelings that provide a definitive yes or no if my rational mind doesn't like the answers. But these are gut feelings. In the past, I purposely ignored these messages because I either didn't want to hear them or I wasn't ready to. They're always there, tapping on my shoulder or giving me a nudge over and over until they become too strong to push aside. Now if intuition insists, I take bold action and push through discomfort, whereas before, I may have brushed it off as a silly thought.

Even though I haven't always acted in alignment with the higher powers directing me on my path, I've felt them strongly throughout my life. I have always known I am here for a reason and that my life is leading somewhere. All I need to do is listen to the inner whispers that keep me on track and trust that I am heading in the right direction.

It's hard to be hopeful and trust in the future when we are not connected to something bigger than ourselves.

No matter what happens to me, I often think of that Jesus statue at Nanna and Pop's and the way he seemed to stare at me wherever I went: *I'm always watching over you. My eyes are following you no matter where you go in this room, or life. I'm here and I will be with you always.*

Just when my world was falling apart, I trusted that the Universe had a plan for me.

I wasn't to know how dramatically everything was about to change and who was about to reappear in my life.

12

RELINQUISHING BLAME

Why did I stay too long in toxic relationships?

This was a question I knew I had to answer before I could enter into another relationship.

I made an appointment with a hypnotherapist to see if she could help me work out the answer. She took me into a deep meditation in which I found myself inside the belly of an Indiana Jones-like pyramid. The only opening was the doorway I entered through. In the centre was an enormous pit of snakes that hissed at me. I felt trapped, as if I couldn't breathe.

'What do you think the snakes represent?' the hypnotherapist asked.

'They are all the excuses I've used. The reasons I stayed.'

'So how are you going to get away from the snakes, Lisa?'

'I'm going to run back through the doorway,' I said, already planning my escape.

'Are you sure that's what you should do?'

'No, I need to look for another way out. I'm going to climb up the wall and find another opening.' In my dream state, I scanned the cave wall. 'I see a tiny dot of light right up at the top of the cave. I need to find a way to reach it,' I said.

It took a while to scale the wall. The beautiful green field was worth the effort. I saw glorious, colourful flowers and a quaint garden with stone bench seats.

Once the time was up, the hypnotherapist guided me up the ten stairs of consciousness until I was back in the room and completely awake.

When we debriefed the session, I saw that I had an extensive list of rehearsed 'reasons to stay,' and that my default pattern was always to go back to the familiarity of discomfort rather than risk a different direction into the unknown.

I was always paralysed by the 'what ifs.' What if I cause him pain? What if his parents think I'm horrible? What if my parents don't approve? What if people judge me for failing again? What if I don't find somewhere to live? What if I don't have enough money to survive? What if I lose friends? What if this is as good as it gets? Every excuse prolonged my misery.

After this session, I wondered, *What if I had the guts to do what felt right and claim my freedom?* That would have been a more constructive *what if*.

I understood that putting someone else's pain before my own was doing wrong by them.

I have never wanted to disappoint anyone. I've never been

scared to be on my own. I am confident being single and independent. As an introvert, I love my own space and company. I don't need others to fuel my energy.

As an empath, the hypnotherapist explained I'd attracted men with narcissistic tendencies without my even knowing it. Empaths literally feel the mental or emotional state of others. I began to understand why I get choked up easily when I'd see or hear about another person's pain. I feel it strongly as if I'm suffering personally. On the other hand, narcissists have an excessive interest or admiration of themselves. They are entitled and feel special, as if the world owes them something. Narcissists are focused on meeting their own needs and don't care who they hurt in the process. They also tend not to take responsibility for their behaviour while blaming everyone else for their lot in life.

Empaths are also typically people pleasers.

What hope did I have?

Over the years I had become an expert in recognising narcissistic as well as *gaslighting* and *controlling* conduct. These names helped me to identify these behaviours as abusive. They were difficult to recognise when it was happening because they're so insidious and I hadn't yet heard of the terms.

In my relationships, I questioned my worth, had to defend myself and felt frustrated without having a clue why. I was always told I was overreacting when all I wanted was peace. I kept wondering why ordinary conversations became inflated so easily. I would keep apologising for who-knows-what and contemplated that maybe I was being oversensitive. But with more information, and a lot of research and reading, I learned that these are the subtle ways the gaslighter intimidates their victim. Now I am able to recognise them quickly.

As I looked back, I felt sad that Adrian's parents and family had only ever seen a 'dumbed down' version of me. They'd never seen my quirkiness or sense of humour because the few times I'd revealed it, I was yelled at on the car ride home.

'What did you mean by what you said to my brother?'

'Why would you tell them that?'

I'd ended up acting like a part of the furniture most of the time. Getting into conversations wasn't worth the post-mortem.

It had been easy to get trapped. It was as if narcissists could sniff out my empathic nature and then latch on to and feed off me.

But as the lights were going on, I realised I needed to delve deeper than just identify the toxic behaviour in my past relationships. I also had to take responsibility for my role. I must have gained something from these relationships too or I wouldn't have stayed.

What could I possibly have gained?

It was hard to admit, but I had a sense of accomplishment when I made my partner feel better. I tapped into my motherly instincts, which gave me a sense of being needed, the way infants need their parents to survive. Even though my partners believed they were dominant, I knew they were insecure, and they'd never leave me – that would have been the death of them. I was their parasitic host, their source of energy.

If this sounds like a perfect situation where both partner's needs are being fulfilled, it's not – over time, bits of the empath's being get chipped away as the narcissist gains more power.

For me, the side effect was a constant drain on my energy. I coasted along, under the radar, as they were never going to encourage me to step up or grow. I could maintain my safe and comfortable routine. As time passed, it seemed more impossible to break away from the co-dependent relationships.

Dr Shefali is an acclaimed author, international speaker and clinical psychologist who says that we tend to focus on the humanitarian aspects and ignore the shadow side to empaths which is afraid to honour their truth, wants to be seen as the 'good' one, avoids conflict, finds it hard to say no and fails to set boundaries.

Tony Robbins believes that it's easier to take massive action when you are pulled towards something pleasurable than when you are trying to push yourself away from pain. Sometimes we don't have enough leverage when we are heading into the unknown.

In relistening to *The Four Agreements,* I was struck by Don Miguel Ruiz's explanation that we put up with abuse from someone else until it exceeds our level of self-abuse.

We can be extremely hard on ourselves, so it takes a lot for it to be bad enough to leave.

I had always just taken the easy road. I wasn't ready to face certain realities, so I'd put up with not being happy.

I'd settled. I had to believe that I was meant to be in those relationships for a good reason and that I had to surrender to the universal timing of things.

Why had I ignored all the warning signs? In my relationships, I cried more often than I laughed, always anticipated the next outburst, never felt free to be myself, felt controlled, was emotionally punished if I didn't adhere to the silent rules and was constantly put down.

I was always happier when Adrian wasn't home. He hated it when I interacted with the world. I felt guilty spending money – money that I'd earned. I felt guilty when I saw friends. I always made excuses for him. I had to pre-empt his reactions and filter my words.

I used to imagine that if he was in an accident, or became ill, I would run the other way. I'm ashamed to admit it because it's so far away from who I really am, but it's the truth.

I finally got to the bottom of it: at the core of my tolerance was my belief that I deserved the treatment I was receiving. I was punishing myself for my affair with Todd – more harshly than the judgements of others – which kept me in a vicious cycle. I finally came to see that when we don't intrinsically believe we are worth a particular salary, or a certain level of happiness in a relationship, we will never invite it into our reality.

I had to discover my own worth before it was possible to break the pattern I was repeating.

For a long time, I didn't realise that by not leaving, I was being selfish. I was putting another person's life and opportunity for happiness on hold as well as mine. I was preventing them from finding more compatible partners when I knew our relationships weren't going to last.

I am not for a moment excusing abusive behaviour. But I must take accountability for the pattern I helped perpetuate. The men I chose behaved badly, but I was complicit in putting up with it and kept going back for more. I kept attracting the same kind of men and didn't realise until many years later how I kept inviting men into my life who made me relive my old trauma.

They highlighted my unhealed parts, which felt familiar no matter how pathological it was. My exes were part of the dance. At the time we were simply immature. Fighting, inner child against inner child. Each encounter broadened my personal growth. In their own way, they were all there for me. I was an unhealed soul hiding out in the company of other unhealed souls. When others validate our suffering instead of challenge us, we get to stay comfortable. It can take a health issue, the death of a loved one, a break-up or other significant life event to snap us out of our patterns and propel us forward.

I only needed *one* good reason to leave. Actually, did I even need a reason? It is my life. I should have ignored the incessant hissing year after year and listened to the calling of my heart. I was never going to find out what was on the other side of the familiar door until I had slammed it shut once and for all.

I don't believe in giving up easily on relationships – even the best partnerships go through times of pain. Some people meet their 'one' early in life. But that wasn't my story. Time is important and precious. Life is too short to spend it with incompatible partners.

There is no need for me to regret any of my past relationships. I chose to be in them. The men I dated did not have to improve or get better – I had to. I had to take responsibility for recognising when it was time to move on. I kept making the same mistake because I wasn't ready to do the work to make the changes in myself. I didn't realise that I wasn't confident enough or ready to put my heart on the line. I hadn't had enough experience or motivation to take the steps I needed to.

In the midst of my confusion, back when I was trying to figure out how to leave Adrian, I was standing in line at a café. The man in front of me wore a biker's leather jacket covered in dozens of badges. One caught my eye: 'Fear is temporary. Regret is permanent.' I felt it hard. I printed those words out and put them above my desk at work. I looked at it every day until I had enough strength to act on them.

Goldfish may choose to swim around, surviving in their confined space until they are found floating lifeless on the surface. That didn't mean I had to. I knew I had to find my way out of the bowl in order to head towards a brighter future.

13

SAYING YES

After I broke up with Adrian, I had no-one to impress or answer to. I didn't need human interaction to feel fulfilled, and when I wasn't working, I caught up on my reading and focused on getting my life back in order. Mum helped me choose a new bed, and I surrounded myself with more plants, books and candles. I felt unrestrained for the first time in years.

I sang a lot at work. I can't imagine how annoying that was.

One day an email pinged as I was in the midst of the chorus of Britney Spears's 'Hit Me Baby One More Time.'

'Come and have a look at this!' I called.

Rachael and Lauren jumped up from their desks and peered over my shoulder. The email was from Mark – the Newcastle Nerd, as he'd been nicknamed by Adrian. It had been seven months since my visit to The Golden Door and I hadn't heard from anyone.

'Ooooh. That's a bit out of the blue,' Rachael said. 'Quick. Reply. And make sure you make it clear that you're not with Adrian anymore.'

Mark's email was chatty – he'd had a good year and been overseas for his daughters' cheerleading competition. He asked after my dad. And Adrian.

'He's checking if you're still with him,' Rachael said.

'Oh, he is not.'

I replied, letting him know I was happy for him, but it had been a hard year for me. I told him about Dad and how I'd broken up with Adrian, and that I was just getting back on my feet. I threw in that my mum had recently surprised me with a new car. Mine was sixteen years old, and she wanted me to have a roadworthy vehicle for the long freeway drive when I visited.

* * *

Mum had handed me the bottle of wine she'd been given when she bought the car, then directed me out the front of the office to where it was parked.

'It's yours,' she said as she handed me the keys.

'What do you mea—'

'I bought it for you. You'll have to drive me home though.'

* * *

After that, Mark and I sent a few emails back and forth. His words were always kind. We discussed catching up for a coffee if I was ever in Newcastle.

Then one day, he mentioned he still had his ex's booking for The Golden Door which he needed to use.

I wanted to visit there again after Christmas and thought how lovely it would be to share the experience with a like-minded person. But I didn't dare reveal this to him. We arranged to catch up for a drink at a pub a few weeks later.

I felt comfortable in Mark's company, as if I already knew him well.

'I bought a special opening deal for a resort in Thailand for two people,' Mark told me that night.

I'm going on that trip. This thought just popped into my head. Of course, I kept it to myself.

A few weeks later, Mark and I had booked a two-bedroom villa at The Golden Door for the following January. Just as friends.

A couple of weeks later, we caught up for lunch – which he paid for – a courtesy I wasn't used to.

Mark was different from any of the men I'd ever dated, and I wanted our friendship to turn into something romantic. But I needed to make sure I wasn't simply falling for the next person who'd come along. I'd done that too many times before.

One night he invited me for dinner at the last minute.

I had less than an hour to get out of my sweaty gym gear and into dinner attire, but there was no time to wash my hair.

I offered to drive us instead of getting a cab. I was used to being in control and taking responsibility.

'No way. You need to relax too and then we can both have a drink,' Mark insisted.

For the first time in my life, someone took the decision-making responsibility out of my hands, and I loved it.

It was officially our first date. He stayed the night.

When my friend Michelle saw us together, she said, 'I've never seen you so relaxed and yourself with anyone before.'

I was falling madly in love.

A couple of weeks later, Mark said, 'You realise there are no guarantees with me. I don't want to hurt you.'

I felt winded. But somehow, I knew things would be okay.

All I said was, 'It's too late.'

I was unencumbered, but he still had to tie up the loose ends with his ex. They weren't yet divorced, and he was worried about his kids. He hadn't introduced them to other women he'd gone out with either. He didn't want to play with their emotions every time he had a date. He wanted to wait until he knew it wasn't a short-term fling. I already knew it wasn't.

In January at The Golden Door, he found his certainty. We had been dating for two months, and it was as if we'd been together for years. We didn't need two bedrooms in our villa.

One evening he showed me an A4 notebook with well-worn edges. He opened it at a page entitled Perfect Partner.

'Here it is. I wrote down what my ideal woman would be like.'

'Oh my god.'

'What?'

'I have a list too.'

Mine was still folded in the accompanying book to my

fortune cards, between the heart and the ring. I like to think that we manifested each other by vibrating on the same frequency. We had both asked the Universe for what we wanted, and the Universe delivered.

Later, we had fun comparing our lists and were excited to tick everything off each other's even though his was a little more X-rated than mine.

After that, we celebrated our first Valentine's Day. Mark wrote a beautiful message in Italian on a card that was delivered to my office with a stunning bunch of twenty-four roses.

Ciao Bella, non vedo l'ora di vederti stasera. Buon San Valentino. Ama la tua anima gemella xxx

(Hi Beautiful, I can't wait to see you tonight. Happy Valentine's Day. Love, your soulmate xxx)

'Wow, he's moving quickly. Soulmates…woo,' Michelle said after helping me translate the message.

We were still in a bubble. Our worlds were yet to cross over.

One night, as I wrapped my arms and legs around him, he told me, 'You know that you are my rose. I see so much that you have to offer. I'm going to have fun peeling off each petal one by one. I've already seen a few come off, but I know there's so much more still in here, beautiful.'

He pressed his entire palm gently against my chest.

All my life, I'd wanted someone to recognise what was inside me.

I felt like Cinderella. Not at the ball, but the stripped-back version before she was transformed. I was turning back into myself, and it was a blessing.

I'd always imagined I was looking for love. But the deeper truth was that I had been searching to be loved when I was being utterly and wholly myself. The bare and unedited me. The one under the makeup and clothes when I was free of any performance.

I had finally met someone with whom I could speak freely and not have to filter my words or alter my behaviour, someone who didn't want me to play small and saw through to my heart.

I wondered whether it was all too good to be true.

14

HAPPY FAMILIES

After Mark and I had been together four months, I'd met his parents and sister. But I hadn't been introduced to the three most important people in his life – his kids: Chloe, Stephanie and Josh, who were twenty, seventeen and fifteen. He suggested getting everyone, including his kids and parents, together on the Easter long weekend.

When is the right time to introduce a new partner? Who can know? It's a balancing act. Mark and I needed enough time and privacy to get to know each other before unsettling everyone unnecessarily. The kids needed to know what was going on in their dad's life. It just had to feel right.

I got up early to help prepare the house and the food.

'You okay?' Mark asked when they were due to arrive.

'It will be good once today is over so the awkwardness can go away.'

'You'll be fine.' He gave me a hug.

When they arrived, I gave them all a kiss on the cheek. I didn't realise Josh would have to bend down. He was fifteen and six feet tall.

Everyone was quiet, but even so – it felt as if something more was going on. I had imagined us all engaging in robust and fun conversations. But whenever I spoke, hardly anyone responded. I didn't know what more to do. My nervousness turned into queasiness. At some point, it began to feel as if none of them was interested in getting to know me. No-one asked me any questions. The air felt tight.

I ended up speaking to Mark and his parents. The hours passed and it wasn't until the last visitor had left that I took a big breath. I wiped away the smile I'd been wearing for the previous few hours.

Mark raised an eyebrow and looked down before he said, 'Well, that didn't go as well as expected.'

'I wasn't sure if you noticed.'

'Hmmm, would be a bit hard not to.'

I felt a little stupid that I hadn't considered this outcome. *So much for everybody loves me*, I mocked myself. I started to clean up to keep busy, feeling as if I'd failed. Everything had been going so well, and now it felt blah. *I knew it was too good to be true.*

'I'm sure it'll get better,' Mark said. 'They just need to get to know you and see what I see.'

Of course, it must have been painful for his kids to see

another woman in their old family home. It had been almost eighteen months since their parents' separation. The kids were all living with their mum who stayed ten minutes away. She hadn't wanted to keep the family home, so Mark moved back in when she moved out after he'd been renting a place with Chloe for twelve months in the neighbouring suburb. Standing in the kitchen where their mum had once cooked dinner, I'd innocently offered them a drink. Had I seemed over the top? Trying too hard? It had been awkward for me too. But I had to trust that with time, things would get easier.

Later that year, Mark took us all to Hamilton Island. We arrived on our own for the first night, then we all spent a few nights together before I went home and left Mark and the kids to have some time alone.

Mark called me while I was waiting at the airport. 'You okay, beautiful?'

'Not really. Do you realise that over the entire weekend, not one person initiated a conversation with me or asked me a question? Not one.'

I wanted to shriek as loudly as I could to release what I'd held in, but I made an effort to keep my composure at the airport. But I burst into tears as soon as I clicked my seatbelt on the plane. I couldn't wait to get home. I imagined they were glad I'd left too.

But despite how hard those early days were trying to become part of Mark's family, I never considered leaving him. Our love was too strong for me to sacrifice. His children had to deal with our relationship in their own way. I hoped my connection with them would improve in time.

We saw more of the kids – especially Stephanie and Josh – over the following months as they stayed with Mark a night or two each week. I was relieved that our interactions became more comfortable over time.

We'll never know what would have happened if I'd had kids too. But Mark had to juggle everyone's emotions and try to keep everyone happy. I never once sensed he was taking anyone's side, and I always felt his strong support of me.

We heard through some of Mark's friends that Gina, his ex, wanted to reconcile with him. I wasn't sure if this was a rumour, but I needed to ask him a question I wouldn't have been brave enough to express a few years earlier.

'I just want you to know that I'm in a good place, and I'm not going to compete…with anyone,' I told Mark.

I wanted him to know how serious I was. I was about to put everything on the line, but I was worth it. I wasn't going to make the same mistakes again. I wasn't going to play games while he decided if he wanted to be with me or his ex.

'If there's even a one percent chance that you might get back with her, I'm out. I won't fight. I can't compete, and I wouldn't do that to your family.'

As I spoke these words, I wasn't afraid of the truth. Even though it would have been crushing, I know I would have left him if he hadn't given me the answer I needed to hear. I had no more time to waste.

Mark drew me in closer and said, 'I'd rather see where this goes.' Then he kissed me deeply.

But despite his reassurance, I still felt like an outsider when other people were around.

'Remember we haven't been happy for a long time. It's not as if this has just happened overnight. I tried everything to save our marriage. For years. It's just hard because it's all new at the moment, but everyone will get used to us being together.'

The next hurdle was Mother's Day at his ex's place. We wouldn't have gone if it were just Gina and the kids, of course; but it was Mark's mum and dad, and his sister and family too.

'Why does it have to be at her house?' I asked.

'I guess she wants to keep control of it.'

It was set up as if everything was the same as it used to be before his break-up, only this time, I was there as 'the extra person.'

I made a plate to take.

What I remember of that day is sitting on the lounge, not saying much. I listened to everyone talking: all the in-jokes and the sharing of memories. I couldn't eat. My stomach was twisted like rope. I kept drinking wine. The only time I got up was when I needed to go to the bathroom.

'You okay, babe?' Mark kept checking in on me.

'Yep.'

I couldn't say how I felt right there and then. I'd have been a blubbering mess. I kept drinking until the moment finally came to leave. It was dark by then. Not long after we arrived back at Mark's, I ran to the bathroom and vomited violently.

Over the day, the family had gravitated to Mark's ex, surrounding her protectively. She was the perceived underdog, and they made sure she felt comfortable and wasn't offended by my presence. But just because I wasn't the one who had lost Mark didn't mean I didn't have feelings. No-one seemed concerned about my emotional wellbeing. We were cautioned by other family members not to speak of current family holidays in front of her because we'd heard whispers that it made Gina feel left out. But it was fine to speak of all the old times before I'd arrived. It seemed one-sided to me.

Mark and I knew our relationship was worth it. Every challenge seemed to strengthen our bond. No-one knew the depth of our love, partly because we'd made a conscious choice not to rub it in anyone's face. We tried to be as respectful as possible. If anyone was hoping to sabotage us, they were going to be disappointed.

15

WELCOMING INTRUDERS

'What's an in...tru...der?' I was six years old, and Dad and I were watching the news.

'Someone who breaks into houses...like a robber,' Dad said. He placed a comforting hand on my thigh and quickly added, 'But we are safe here and the house is all locked up. You know I wouldn't let anything bad happen to you.'

I managed half a smile. All I knew was that intruders were baddies.

To Gen Y and Gen Z, an intruder is the extra person brought in halfway through reality TV shows: *Big Brother*, *I'm a Celebrity...Get Me Out of Here*, *The Bachelor*. They've all had them. The introduction of an intruder is a tool used by scriptwriters to unsettle the comfort zone of the original contestants to keep viewers captivated. It works every time. The presence of an intruder stirs the pot just as complacency sets in and the contestants have established their unique position in the group. *How dare they create drama and ruin the harmony?*

Not only do intruders turn the previously predictable environment upside down, they also open old wounds and expose the flaws and insecurities of the original contestants. To intrude is to thrust, or bring in, with no invitation, permission or welcome. It's expected that the 'new' person will be rejected.

In the early days of our relationship, I was watching an episode of *The Bachelor*. A group of the original contestants was sitting in the garden, all dressed up and plastered with makeup. As they sipped on sparkling wine in anticipation of the rose ceremony, one woman said, 'I'll be really angry if one of us leaves before the intruders.'

'When do they stop being intruders and just become people like the rest of us?' one of the others asked.

The conversation triggered a moment of realisation in my own life. *I'm an intruder. That's it.*

I'd never known how to express how I felt as the new person in my relationship with Mark, but this made so much sense. As I watched the women attempt to alienate the intruders, I got goosebumps. All the intruders wanted was to fit in; at the same time, the originals were desperately trying to lock them out. The intruders were not welcome and were treated as if they were inferior – somehow disconnected from the rest because they arrived a little later. On *The Bachelor*, the latecomers were never fully accepted and were typically sent home before the end. *Voila.* Gone. It was as if the temporary gate crashers had never existed.

I felt as if some people hoped the same would happen to me – that I would eventually go away, be voted off. What period of time needed to pass in my relationship with Mark before I went from being an intruder to just like anyone else? I had to accept that I might never be anything else. Forever an intruder.

But I found it increasingly difficult to deal with the unsettled energy I felt at family gatherings. I'm a radar for lost souls, the one who scans events for those who appear marginalized and uncomfortable so I can make them feel included. So when I wasn't made to feel welcome, it caught me off balance.

I also had a past life with family and partners pre-Mark. I could only share Mark's experiences from the time we met. There is no equivalent of catch-up TV for life. Mark's close family and friends knew his history and life BL (Before Lisa). They didn't miss season one of the series like I had. They had their place in the inner circle with all the other originals, and I struggled sensing some would be happier without me there. All I'd done was meet a wonderful man and fall in love, but I was treated as if I'd purposely barged in unannounced to create havoc. I had been labelled before they took the time to get to know me. I was isolated, ignored and punished for being brought in later. But this wasn't a TV show. It was my reality. Judged for bad timing, even though Mark and I knew that our timing couldn't have been better.

It's frightening how many hours I wasted feeling troubled, anxious and frustrated. I craved an unrealistic one-hundred-percent approval rating. The perfectionist in me has never been satisfied unless every single person likes me. I invested a disproportionate amount of time and energy in feeling rejected and dismissed by a few, and not enough in embracing the love and welcome I received from the majority.

The first time I met Tiffany, a close friend of Gina's, she laughed as she said, 'Damn it. I wanted to hate you, but I don't.'

I was appreciative whenever any of Mark's friends and family made space for me.

But I tended to focus on a negative few because in an inexplicable way, it gave me proof that my limiting beliefs about myself were correct. It only took one person to validate and reawaken those hard-wired beliefs. One person's resistance was enough to re-evoke the feeling that I wasn't enough; I wasn't worthy.

I had to contend with everyone's attempts to be loyal to their friends and family while dismissing how rejected this made me feel.

I could see that Mark's family and some of his close friends were grieving for a time past and wanted to press pause on me to make space for the changes happening around them. Perhaps they felt disloyal to Gina and imagined that by accepting a new person, it would imply they'd rejected the old. But there's no upper limit on love. It doesn't need to be taken from someone and handed over to someone else. It is extra, not 'instead of.'

I also became an easy scapegoat to blame for old family issues.

Over these tricky months, I came to learn as an intruder that the only power I had was to trust – myself and the process. I had to believe that if I remained true to myself and survived the gossip, judgement and disrespect, I may, over time, be seen as the person I am instead of the fictional one conjured up in other peoples' minds. How I was being treated had nothing to do with me. It had to do with everyone's ability (or inability) to cope with change. They were hurting too. They say, 'Hurt people, hurt people,' but I think it's a horrible sentiment and unleashes terrible karma. I don't agree that being hurt is a valid justification to behave badly towards others. Haven't we all been hurt? It doesn't give us all the right to pass on our pain and inflict it on others.

Intruders are not just robbers or extras on reality TV shows. They could be the new kid at school, the latest recruit at work, the second spouse or the immigrant who's just arrived, all just hoping to make a fresh start, wanting to belong. We are all connected. We are all the same. Our circumstances are sure to change.

We will all have our turn at being an intruder. Until then, it is honourable to welcome and accept the people who come into our lives later and not punish them for not being there first.

16

SPUNKY SPIRIT

'Do you have any regrets?' I asked Mum a few years ago.

We were sitting at my dining room table, and I was questioning her as part of research for this book.

'In what way?'

'Like, if you had your time over again, would you like to have done something in your life or career you missed out on?'

Mum paused before answering. 'I just wanted to have you kids. I took thirteen years off to look after you until you were old enough for me to go back to work.'

'Is there nothing you would have loved to have done?'

'Not really. I wanted to have my own family…and for it not to be anything like my childhood. I suppose I could have done something in forensics or something like that. I love all those shows. That may have been interesting. But, ah, no. I've done everything I wanted to.'

She pursed her lips and looked as though she was still considering my question. I'm not sure if she was trying to convince me or herself.

Like Mum, I assumed that one day I'd get married and have kids. *That's why we're here, isn't it?*

Unlike Mum, who hadn't had ambitions beyond the house, I'd always wanted to *do* something impactful. I dreamt of coming up with ingenious inventions, being a famous television personality or a highly successful businesswoman. So why hadn't I?

Once in Newcastle, while Mark and I were heading to the beach, a mother and a young boy headed towards us. The boy was hunched over and moving as if being dragged. His thongs squeaked along the concrete.

'No,' his mother was saying. 'We're not going in there. There are monsters in there. We're going over here instead because there are no monsters in there.' She pointed to the ocean baths.

'But—'

'It's like a big pool.'

I watched her try to sell the baths to the boy the way a real estate agent points out all the obvious features. *This is the kitchen. Oh, really, I would have never guessed.*

I felt sorry for the poor kid. He was going to miss out on so much fun in his life if he developed a genuine fear of scary beach monsters in the surf.

A few hours earlier on our morning walk, I was trying to

teach Mark a glute-tightening exercise when a pink and yellow flash interrupted us. It was a little girl zooming on her pink scooter with her matching helmet ahead of us. She couldn't have been more than two years old. My eyes followed her tiny frame and shoulder-length white-blond hair. She rode a hundred metres from her mum without looking back.

'*She's* not scared,' I said as we passed the mum.

'She's hard to keep up with. That's why I have to wear these clothes,' she smiled, gesturing to her active wear.

The little girl stopped and was talking to people and patting their dogs. She turned back only once to check that her mum was still there. She finally stopped when she reached the base of a steep hill, chatting up a couple of walkers as she waited.

I wondered when I had lost the free spirit I saw in her.

When I was that age, I'd stayed close to Mum or Dad, not letting them out of my sight. Talking to strangers was a no-no, and I'd bury myself behind Mum's or Dad's legs to avoid having to do so. I would never pat scary dogs. 'Dad, lift me up,' I'd say if a dog was coming anywhere near me.

We weren't allowed a dog as a pet, so they were alien to me. They were messy and unpredictable, and not welcome in the house. (Dirt and dust weren't allowed in either.) Mum would never have been able to deal with feeding a dog, cleaning up its poo or washing it. I was taught to think of them as germ carriers that would give me worms or ticks if I got too close. Neither Mum nor Dad had dogs when they grew up either. Fish were easy. We had a few of those over the years. They just swam around within the four glass walls which contained them. Except Rocket. He was a rebel fish who mustn't have liked being restrained because one day, he jumped out onto the 'babyshit yellow' Laminex benchtop as Dad used to call it.

We had plenty of birds in an aviary Dad built – more than eighty at one stage. He bred them and used to enter them in competitions. Budgie meetings were once a month. Sometimes he won prizes. It was the size of the head that counted. The ones that looked funny and top-heavy were the prize-winners for some reason. A couple of times, I watched Dad clip the wings of the ones we kept as pets. That way, we could let them out in the house without worrying they would fly away. We used to feed them cornflakes.

Hewy was our favourite. He still had both his wings and he could talk. Mum was funny to watch when he pooed on the furniture or the carpet.

'Ke-en, catch Hew—'

'He's all right.'

'Get him out of here!'

Kim and I giggled once as Hewy flapped around and landed on my head. His claws tickled and gave me goosebumps.

Cute and clever as they are, you can't hug or snuggle up with a bird or a fish. All of this conditioning left its marks on me.

It's impossible to escape the imprints of how we are parented. Our upbringing impacts on who we become as people.

How much of who I'd become as an adult had to do with my genetic makeup, and how much with my environment and conditioning?

Every parent was once a child with parents who influenced them. We all grow in an endless connection of solid rings that make up the trunk of the family tree.

Mum was adamant that she would never pressure us to excel or do something we didn't want to because she was so affected by the demands put on her by her own parents.

'Being pushed made me want to give up and not try as hard,' I often heard her say.

Some parents repeat the mistakes of their own parents, which perpetuates negative cycles. Others replicate what their parents did successfully and reject what failed. They attempt to fix the problems of their own childhood in those of their children.

Doing the opposite of what your parents did can be equally as destructive as copying them because it assumes your child is just like you. But every single child needs to be loved in a different way, depending on their personality, environment they were brought up in as well as their unique set of experiences.

Gary Chapman's book, *The Five Love Languages,* explains this concept beautifully. Everyone craves love in a different form, and each of us develops a primary love language. We feel loved when we receive physical connection, quality time, acts of service, spoken words or gifts. If you are giving your child the things *you* missed out on growing up, aren't you attempting to fulfil your own needs, not theirs?

Mum didn't push me to study or obtain high grades because she didn't want to put me through the pain she'd felt as a child. But maybe I would have benefitted if I'd been pushed harder. It was easy for me to stay in the safe zone as a child and young adult but doing so exacerbated my fears and filtered through to the way I approached life as an adult. I would have benefitted from being encouraged to break through and out.

Mark has frequently and kindly pushed me into discomfort, and this has helped me transform and grow. This is exactly what Mum complains her parents did to her. Does that make her wrong? No, just different. She was never going to push us because to her, that wasn't good parenting.

Our inbuilt bias for negativity tends to make us critical of our parents for their shortfalls. But it's never the full story – they have likely also made huge sacrifices. Talking to my mum made me more empathic about her parenting style and allowed me to imagine living in the world she came from.

Before the internet, Google and continuous stimulation from social media, our parents had to learn from their parents who didn't even have a television set, let alone the world wide web. They learnt by passing things on. It was a slow process. They had no instant, accessible information and a limited awareness of the environment and conservation.

Carl Jung wrote, 'The greatest burden a child must bear is the unlived life of its parents.'

Each of us lives out this quote in our own way.

The little girl on the scooter wasn't fearful as she discovered the giant world with no limitations. I, like the little boy, was pulled in to conform. I understand that the way I was brought up – with the best intentions by both my loving parents – influenced my interpretation of the world. But in developing an unhealthy fear of everything, a part of me got lost.

Kim and I were Dad's girls. He protected and looked after us. As a result, we missed out on experiences. Kim was the 'son he never had' and spent more time with her in the outdoors while I spent indoor time with Mum. She, the tomboy – me, the princess – each seeking approval from one parent. Kim craved Dad's approval, and I craved Mum's. Kim said that she and Dad used to have conversations about the fish they'd caught. The victory of their success was always dampened by the anticipation of Mum's crankiness when they returned as she dealt with their stinky clothes and the mess, as well as the hassle of having to fillet, batter and cook the fish which she was always proud to present in perfect cocktail-sized pieces.

We felt safe and loved. But we were constantly on alert – ever aware, hypervigilant – so as not to upset Mum.

It's not like we were kept in a fish tank or an aviary. We were allowed to venture out of our yard. We rode bikes in the street and played with the neighbours, but we were never too far away from the confines of the eight-hundred-square-metre block. Without ill intent, keeping us so close had the same effect on his girls as Dad's clipping of the wings had on his budgies. We were held back from soaring and reaching our full potential. Instead, we flapped around in a circle, using up a lot of energy but getting nowhere.

17

TAKING RISKS

After hearing the forecast, we presumed the local Saturday yacht race would be cancelled, but the committee had other plans. Full wet-weather gear was rare in November. I could barely recognise the men behind the jackets, overalls, boots and gloves, their alert eyes peering through the gaps in their hoods. *Mojo* rocked us like a cradle over the choppy, rough conditions while we waited for the start.

'*Watch for the flag!*' Mark bellowed, gripping the wheel with both hands. He knew the whistling wind would swallow the fire of the gun. Holding onto the rail a little tighter than normal, I was unsure what to expect. People were speaking only to scream out orders. No idle chit-chat today.

'*One minute!*' I screamed as loudly as I could as I barely

made out the big black dot on the yellow flag being pulled down on the start boat.

I was in charge of the countdown to the start. I raised one finger in the air for Fletchie, who lifted his hand to his ear on the bow. In four years, it was the first time I'd seen the main sail reefed in preparation for the gale-force winds.

I confirmed the timer on my iPad was in sync at the one-minute mark. I started yelling out every ten seconds until we got to the final thirty seconds. I'm not sure if anyone heard me – I was right behind Mark as I yelled from '*Thirty seconds*' down to '*Three… Two… One… Go!*' using my biggest voice. Luckily, I had the iPad because I didn't see the yellow start flag come down. Suddenly, yachts appeared through the mist on each side as we all tried to get to the best position on the starting line. I felt the adrenaline surging through my body. We took off ahead of the pack, but it was more about finishing the race in one piece than winning it that day.

Some boats in the fleet headed back to the marina within the first hour of the race with shredded sails or broken masts. I squeezed the rail even harder as the lightning and thunder chased us. Daylight appeared to be switched off, except when the sky lit up with each bloodcurdling strike. I bounced as each one crackled.

'Woohoo!' Mark shouted. He was in his element.

This is what sailors live for. Like surfers who wait for the huge swells, they get excited by fifty-knot winds.

'*Squall coming!*'

This must be serious, I thought, as the other nine crew members brought down the main sail at a frightening pace. The rain hammered our jackets as the waves smashed well over the port deck. In the heart of the southerly, among the chaos and ferocity of the wildest storm, I kept my composure. I was still. My breath was even. Overcome by being in the hands of the powerful sea, I had to surrender. My job was to hold on tight while capturing the whole experience on the iPad.

I trusted Mark, I trusted *Mojo* and I trusted the experienced crew. Together they had battled several Sydney to Hobart races, and all I needed to do was grip the pole and take in the surreal moment. My arm was the only brace keeping me from falling headfirst into the water as *Mojo*'s deck became almost vertical and my stomach was left behind. As I came face to face with the water, I wondered how the keel could possibly be the only thing stopping us from tipping right over. But *Mojo* thrived in these conditions and, sure enough, she straightened up. As the storm passed over and Mother Nature retreated, the sun returned, along with a few laughs and nervous sighs.

I had heaps of annual leave accrued, so in our first year together, I was able to accompany Mark on a cruise to nowhere, a long weekend in Darwin, a work trip to New Zealand and, as I'd intuited, that pre-booked trip to Thailand. We had only been together for five months, and both got severe food poisoning at the five-star resort. We got to know each other very well very quickly as we tag-teamed in and out of the bathroom with our insides being purged from both ends. I actually thought I might die over there. Mark managed to negotiate a free holiday for the following year when we found out there were dozens of other people poisoned at the same meal at the resort. We can laugh about it now, but at the time, it was impossible to lift our heads without vomiting.

From Darwin, we visited Litchfield National Park; and apart from the crocodile jumping cruise, I was most looking forward to swimming in the waterhole at the base of Florence Falls. I'd always wanted to swim under a waterfall.

When we arrived, Mark grabbed my hand, ducked his head under the water, pulling me with him. I wrapped my legs around his waist and he kissed me tenderly. He looked me right in the eye and said, 'Do you wanna?'

I didn't think it was possible to have sex under water, but I was proven wrong. I felt reckless and uninhibited, not worrying about the other people there or whether I'd get in trouble. I was enveloped in the moment and dwarfed by the power of the water falling beside us. Mark was showing me how to be free. I was a quick learner.

Sometimes I fell back into old habits. Like the time Mark called and asked me to change my regular hair appointment because he had tickets to the Hunter Valley Gardens Christmas Lights show. It was meant to be spectacular. From the advertising I'd seen, it looked like a magical fairyland where everything was completely covered in vibrant and colourful lighting.

I was tempted, but how could I cancel my standard Thursday-night hair appointment scheduled every six weeks? If I did:

I'd have to go out with filthy hair and wear it in a ponytail;

I'd have to fit the haircut into another time that would upset my schedule;

I'd have to rush home and pack quickly;

I'd have to drive straight to work the next morning, so I'd need to organise work clothes; and

I'd have to find something to wear. *Argh.*

'Well, if you change your mind, let me know. I've never been, but I've heard it's really good,' Mark said.

Rachael and Lauren insisted I call the hairdresser and simply change the appointment. Even though it was such late notice, my hairdresser happily rescheduled; and suddenly, I was free for the evening.

As I drove up the freeway, I felt naughty. It was becoming a habit. Mark pushed my boundaries and encouraged me to do things I would have never done previously. Being with him helped me redraw some of those ridiculous patterns I was enslaved to.

The Christmas Lights display was magical, filled with characters, animals, butterflies, plants, rainbows and candy canes made out of the luminous glow of the lights. We walked under canopies dripping with fairy lights as tree trunks and branches were lit up. It was wondrous, like a childhood dream.

To think that I might have missed this for a hair appointment.

I was beginning to feel safe to let my guard down completely. And life was the most exciting it had ever been.

18

CHILDLESS WOMAN

Perhaps because I feared getting into trouble, I didn't often succumb to peer pressure. I didn't drink alcohol during my school years even though it was fashionable, and I didn't get a tattoo even though all of my uni friends did on a road trip to Byron Bay in the nineties. I held on to my own opinions and wouldn't get swayed by the collective thoughts of the group. Sometimes it's tough being the outlier. Never more so than being a woman without children.

I love kids.

But I've gone against the norm, and I've never had children. I've overridden biological imperatives and instinctive hard wiring. American biologist Bruce Lipton explained in a talk at the Hay House Summit a few years ago that there are two types of survival biologically built into humans: the survival of the individual and the survival of the species through reproduction.

It's in our genes to procreate, so my decision is hard for others to comprehend. I've gone against societal expectations. As little girls, most of us grow up anticipating the day we'll get married and have a family. I was the girly girl with all the dolls, training to be a mother before my body had the capacity to become one. I'd always wanted to be a mother. *Or was I brainwashed by all that pre-programming?*

I thought by the age of twenty-six, I'd have a husband and three or four kids. I made this prediction in my commerce class in Year Ten, when we were asked to write down what our life would look like in the year 2000. Though I was still a teenager, I had never considered *not* having children. Not once. But being anything other than a mother was never offered as an alternative.

Dad always reminded me I have childbearing hips – an inappropriate comment by today's feminist standards. I wasn't taught that you could choose whether to have children or not. No-one thought twice when they said, 'When you have kids,' or 'You'll know what it's like when you have your own.' These days, people are more open-minded. But in my generation, it was assumed there must be something wrong with you – physically or emotionally – if you didn't go the motherhood route.

But not having kids doesn't make one anti-kids.

Even into my forties, I was always questioned (interestingly only by women) and expected to justify my choice. For years, I'd get asked at least once a month. Now as I move closer to fifty, the invasive curiosity has waned, but those who still ask seem desperate to make sense of my response.

'I didn't meet the right man until it was a bit late,' I say, which is my way of moving onto another conversation. Everyone seems to want another, better reason, one they can digest and relate to. This results in ridiculous explaining from me, making me sound superficial and contrived.

Some offer up solutions for my 'problem.' 'Oh, it's not too late. You're still young.'

Everyone has an example of someone they know who had a baby in their forties. I understand they are searching for a way to connect with me. Maybe they feel sorry for me and don't want me to miss out on the joy they've experienced. It is exhausting though.

I can't recall a conversation amongst women where they must account for their reasons for choosing to have a baby. No explanation is needed. It is 'normal' and natural. Imagine for a moment having to explain, on a monthly basis, why you made your choice to have children.

'But why did you really have kids? Okay, but can you give me a better reason? Oh, are you sure it's the right decision? You might regret those kiddies one day. I hope they don't neglect you when you're older. What could your life have been like without them? Is it what you expected? Did you think long and hard before you decided to make a decision that is going to affect you for the rest of your life?'

Childless women experience this type of unsolicited cross-examination all the time. It's nothing but adult peer pressure. Not to mention how crushing the interrogations would have been if I had tried to have children and couldn't.

I recently found a journal from my mid-twenties in which I wrote: *How could I bring a tiny human into this scary and unpredictable world of chaos and disorder? How could I possibly be responsible for and protect a precious life when so much could go wrong?*

I'd also had strange intuitive feelings and premonitions through my twenties and thirties about having difficulty in, or not surviving, childbirth. I'm not sure whether that was a coping mechanism or a justification, or whether it was a real warning to me. I'll never know.

When Mark and I first started going out, he was quick to ask, 'How do you feel about kids?'

'I love them. I always thought I would have my own, but things don't always turn out the way we plan, huh?'

'Do you still want to have a baby?'

'I would have if I was a bit younger, but I don't really want to be dealing with teenagers when I'm sixty. I would probably have had them by now if I'd have been with the right man.'

'I just want to make it clear from the outset that if you're looking for a father for a baby, that's probably not going to happen here. You'd be surprised how many women in their thirties are desperately looking for that.'

When we met, I was nearly forty, and Mark's three children were adolescents and young adults.

'I get it, and that's not me. I've always believed that I need to be happy within myself first, then if I meet a wonderful man, it's a bonus. The decision to have children depends on the individual couple. Every situation is different. Men or babies won't fix your problems. You can't just look for someone to father your kids, or you'll compromise your relationship, which is more important to me. I know it's not a mainstream opinion, but that's how I feel.'

I'd rattled it off so many times I didn't know whether I believed it myself.

'Exactly,' Mark said. 'Kids highlight the problems that are already there.'

'A lot of women are desperate to have children, so they look for a man to fulfil that need. No wonder there are so many break-ups when the kids grow up. The focus was on children instead of the relationship. Thank you for being so honest,' I said.

I didn't make the decision about becoming a mother before I met my life partner. To me, that is not the natural order. It's like beginning to drive somewhere before you know the address you're heading to. Whilst I was with men with whom I couldn't see a future, I was never going to have a baby with them. I waited until I found the partner I wanted to be with for the rest of my life, and then we talked about children based on our circumstances. If I'd been younger, it would have been another kind of conversation; and if I'd met someone younger who didn't already have kids of their own, I'm sure it would have been a different conversation too. But that wasn't how it was.

We had countless conversations over the next several months as our relationship became more serious. With all the quizzing from Mark, I became more curious about how I really felt. I needed to make sure I wasn't placating him. No, I'd never had the ticking biological clock that everyone talks about. No, I'd never had a desperate *need* to have kids, and the thought of *not* having them didn't upset me. My tears are always a pretty good barometer for the truth too. When things don't sit right with me, I can't help but get emotional. I wasn't emotional about this decision.

Don't get me wrong. I do get emotional when I witness babies being born or see special connections between mothers and their children. It's natural to wonder *what if*. It's a special and unique bond I will never have. But I also cry when people sing beautifully, dance from their soul, lose family, or battle serious illness or hardship. I feel the full spectrum of emotions in other people. It's not because I'm regretful – it's because of who I am. I feel other people's joy as well as their sorrow.

Once I'd gotten clear inside myself that I was being truthful, Mark surprised me several months later when he said, 'I know we've done this talk about babies to death, but I've been doing a lot of thinking. And I love you so much that if you really want to have a baby, I don't want you to miss out.'

'That's the absolute last thing I expected you to say.' I paused and took a sip of wine. 'That really means a lot to me. I've told you my view on this though. Nothing has changed.'

'I know. I just don't want you to –'

'I know. It's not just about me though. You've just finished raising your kids, and you'd be starting again. Your whole life would be just about raising kids.'

'But you haven't had that experience. I don't want to be the one to take that from you.'

'I get that. Thank you. Let's talk about it later, but I feel the same as I have the last thousand times we've talked about it. I promise.'

'I don't want you to resent me later on.'

I promised him I wouldn't, and I never have.

I'm not sure what would have happened if I'd have said yes. All I know is that Mark didn't want to feel responsible for me losing the opportunity to have children because of him. It made me love him even more.

I thought about the women who think they'll change their partner's mind after enough time has passed. I thought about the ones who didn't have the 'baby conversation' until they were married. I thought about those who desperately want to have babies but can't.

Was I being selfish? Or selfless? What was my truth? Why had I given up my chance to have a child? It's a decision many women don't believe I've freely chosen. If I couldn't explain it to myself, no wonder I find it impossible to explain to others.

But then, isn't everyone missing out on something? We always sacrifice something when we make a choice. For every decision we make, there is something we have denied. Mothers are missing out too: on eight hours sleep a night, the ability to go out for dinner on the spur of the moment or to take carefree holidays. In sailing, one minute you can be travelling along beautifully when the wind is behind your sail, and the next minute you're going nowhere fast. There is no right or wrong. Whatever we decide has both positive and negative consequences. But it's natural to contemplate what's on the other side of the fence.

Some of us are not meant to be biological mothers. I know I am a mother to many anyway. I am also a mother to my plants, and I'm birthing something unique into the world with this book. I have inbuilt maternal instincts, and I know I'll call on them throughout my life. I believe we choose our parents because we have something to learn from them. No-one ultimately owns their kids. Parents are caretakers, and their main job is to prepare their children for their own lives and to equip them to make their own decisions. I may never experience being a mum firsthand in this life, but I know I have another purpose to fulfil.

Not having children has given me the opportunity to dedicate a huge amount of time to consciousness work and to do this sooner than many who are busy with their children. I am forever grateful for that. By investing this time, I hope I can help the next generation in other ways.

By choosing to continue my relationship with Mark, I sacrificed my last chance to have a baby. I gave up children, but I gained something precious too. I found my person. My twin flame. A man who sees me. A man I love and who loves me for me. Someone who wants me to be all that I can be. I may never hear the words, 'Your child is gorgeous,' but many people have remarked about me and Mark that 'You guys have great energy,' which means the world to me. If I'd been set on having a baby, I could have thrown it all away in the early days and may never have found such a deep and true connection. I don't regret my choice. If I were meant to be a mother, I would have met someone who wanted kids earlier. I couldn't imagine my life without Mark, but I can imagine life without kids. I don't need to imagine it. It's a reality. You can't miss what you've never had.

Thank goodness women have alternatives these days. We get to walk our own paths and choose whether we even want a partner at all. We get to decide to have a career and if we want to have children. Whatever choice we make deserves respect. We all have to embrace our lives, whether they involve a career, partner, children or any combination of these.

I've never had a problem with not having children, but the rest of the world seems to. Others have tried to convince me that it is a big deal, but it isn't. Of course, my story is only my story – this may not be the case for other women.

I believe everything unfolds exactly as it is meant to, and I will continue to be grateful for what I do have and not focus on what I don't. I'm also proud that I still possess the courage to do what is right for me – to not conform just because *everybody else is doing it*.

19

MY OLD LIFE

When I moved from the Central Coast to Newcastle to live with Mark, I gave up the security and comfort of my old life as I knew it. But I was also giving up predictability and complacency. The scales tipped in favour of opportunity, even as I had to make sacrifices. Nothing I gave up felt like a loss. I felt aligned with the timing.

I was nervously excited for the fresh start. I would be further away from some close friends and have to travel an hour each way to and from work, but I'd commuted to Sydney for seven years, which was double the distance. I could manage it.

For the first time, I was in a relationship with someone I loved unconditionally. I had no doubt that I was going to stick around for Mark no matter what. It wouldn't matter whether one of us was sick, how much money we had or where we were living. As long as we were both alive, we would be there for each other. I was free of niggling doubts and could detect not a single warning sign. It was a completely new territory for me.

My friends said, 'He's a male version of you.'

His friends told me they'd never seen him happier. Of course, I couldn't see the impact I'd had on him. To me, he'd always been happy. We clicked. We were locked in. We met exactly when we were meant to. *Thank you, divine timing.*

I probably fell for Mark first. He was more guarded in the beginning. I didn't have kids, and nothing in my past was weighing me down.

Five months into our relationship, we were lying against each other, skin to skin, in the fresh light of the morning sun. I had one arm around his stomach and was staring at him when he leaned his head towards me and said, 'I love you.'

Just like that. No warning.

'I love you too.'

I'd been waiting to hear him say this but hadn't been focused on if and when. I was never going to say it to Mark first because I was making a conscious effort not to be the one directing the relationship. I wanted him to step up in a way that no other man had for me.

I'd never heard my mum or dad say, 'I love you,' even though I knew they must have. I didn't need verbal confirmation. Mark's love for me was everywhere. I secretly knew.

It was only natural that we'd end up moving in together. I was spending more and more time at Mark's place, and my unit became an expensive storage facility. I rented it out. Even though my friends and job were on the Central Coast, his kids and his whole family were in Newcastle, as was Saturday sailing. Most of my family had left the area by then, so it was a no-brainer that I would be the one to move.

Then on Valentine's Day 2015, we signed the contract on our own home. It wasn't his old family home. It wasn't his, it wasn't mine. It was *ours*. Around the same time, a new job came up for Mark based in Sydney. When I met him, his job was in Newcastle even though he was looking after businesses all around Australia and overseas.

It wasn't always easy for me to keep up with the pace of his life. There was always something on – work trips, social events, family catch-ups. He was used to it, but I wasn't.

Mark was seriously considering the new job as the CEO / Managing Director of a company in Sydney as the next step in his career, and I wanted to support him.

My mind started micro-managing all the different scenarios. If he took the job and we moved to Sydney, I would have to do the laborious Sydney / Central Coast commute again, just in the opposite direction. Moving again. Packing. There was a tornado in my brain.

'It's a big role so I'd need your help. You wouldn't be able to stay in your job if we do this. We'd be going back and forth between Sydney and Newcastle, and it would be a team effort.'

Oh.

My identity had always been wrapped up in my independence. I still had savings in the bank and an income from my property, but the thought of not having income deposited into my account each week made my skin clammy. I had worked with some of my closest friends for thirteen years, and the office was like a family. Was I ready to leave it? Did I even want to? Tough as it was to admit, I was not mentally stimulated at work and hadn't been for a long time. I had settled for comfort and security over growth. Here I was again, being nudged into making a change I should have instigated years earlier.

I'd always been the one in charge. Here I was being asked to let go of control, to trust someone else for a change, to not have to be the one responsible for everything even though I'd always done it all.

'Maybe you could work on that book you've been wanting to write,' Mark suggested.

Now he had my attention. It was something I'd wanted to do for years, imagining it as a hobby, not something I could devote myself to full time.

I would never have chosen to move to Sydney. I'd commuted each day all those years ago when my work was there. I wondered if the people pleaser in me had returned.

No, this time I was supporting my partner to realise his dream which, in turn, meant that I could focus on mine. It didn't take long to accept it as an exciting plan. Mark and I convinced ourselves that this next chapter would be a positive experience for us. We embraced it as an adventure we'd look back on and say, 'How amazing that we did that.'

And then it got hard.

We heard the story doing the rounds that I was the reason Mark was being *taken away* from his kids. Though we planned to return to Newcastle every weekend, I became the scapegoat again. It was tough to realise I was always going to be blamed because I was the intruder.

One of his kids asked me about the move, one day when we were alone in the kitchen, and suggested that I was the one behind the move.

'You have your sister down there, don't you? And one of your best friends.'

'Yes, that's true.' My sister and friend did live in Sydney, but we were moving there because of Mark's career.

'Well, his family is here,' came back the bitter reply.

Mark was in the garage and wasn't there to set the record straight. Later, when he asked why I was crying, I told him about the conversation. He was always so supportive and wasn't worried what anyone else thought. But I was the one under scrutiny, not him.

'It's not fair. They still believe stories that aren't even true.'

'It's not worth worrying about. You know you can't win. You just have to ignore it.'

We began our double life, but not before moving into our new home in Newcastle, celebrating Mum's sixty-fifth birthday with a big party at her place (Dad had been critically ill for her sixtieth so it was an important one), a road trip on the Great Ocean Road in Melbourne with the kids, followed by three weeks overseas. We went to Venice and Rome then hired a boat on the Canal du Midi in France. We went on to Paris and finished up in New York, which included a day trip to Niagara Falls. Mark had to take advantage of the break between jobs. We had so much fun. We both felt free after leaving our long-term roles.

Our Sydney home was far enough away from the epicentre that it didn't even feel like we were in a big city. We promised to see it as an adventure and, boy, did we have fun enjoying the best of both worlds. We had date nights at different restaurants, ferry trips into town, and attended shows and events.

'I would have never been able to do this before,' Mark said a few months into the new job.

'And I would never have been able to do *this*.'

'We're a good team,' he said.

I winked at him. 'We certainly are.'

Mark never once made me feel as if I was not pulling my weight. If he had, my instant reaction would have been to go straight back to full-time work. I did do some ad hoc work supporting other writers for my writing mentor's business. I had passionate and inspirational conversations with women about her courses, and I assisted at her workshops and loved every minute of it. It was a new experience to not be in charge of everything for a change, and the beautiful connections I made were invaluable for my emotional and personal development.

I'd been in control of the finances when I was with Adrian. Each week, he'd give me his pay so I could organise the bills, budget and save. I had to write down every cent I spent, right down to each hot chocolate or lip balm. Back then, I didn't know what financial abuse was. Adrian never took control of the finances or assets, or spent money on my credit card – these are some typical signs of financial abuse. But there was a double standard when it came to spending. He didn't support me advancing my career so I could earn more money. It would have made him feel inferior. I'm still not sure whether I experienced financial abuse. But I accepted – and colluded in – behaviour that wasn't healthy. While I was being frugal and writing every expenditure down in my little black book, Adrian would spend hundreds of dollars on protein powders, gym shoes and muscle singlets from overseas.

I used to feel guilty when I spent any money even though I was the main breadwinner, so when the only income I had was the rent from my unit, I became positively frugal. I spent money only when absolutely necessary and used my own savings for writing courses.

Rumours trickled back that Mark's friends referred to me as 'a lady of leisure at forty' and made jokes about my being 'retired so young.' Another one said, 'Wow, I'd love to be retired at her age.' No wonder I kept having tight pain in my chest and felt on the verge of tears so often. It was fruitless to try explaining myself.

The truth is, writing was the hardest work I'd ever done. But sometimes I just allowed myself to cry freely when I was alone or with Mark. To outsiders, I may have appeared not to care what people thought, but I did. I was desperate for acceptance, and it hurt that I couldn't defend myself. No-one knew that I contributed thousands of dollars to those early holidays, and significant amounts to our joint home loans and, more recently, our motorhome.

I was judged because I wasn't working, and there was not a damn thing I could do about it. I was distraught that his friends thought I was mooching off him. I had been proud of my independence. If only they knew the full story. Giving up control and my financial independence was one of the hardest changes I have ever made.

But what I got in return helped me grow.

I crammed more living into my years with Mark than I had in the previous four decades of my life.

PART THREE
Shutting Up

20

UNEXPECTED VISITORS

Travelling the two-hour commute between Newcastle and Sydney every week was fun but gruelling. For the first four and a half years, we rarely slept at one place for more than five days in a row. The first eighteen months in Sydney we lived in a unit; the next five years we lived on our boat. It sounds glamorous, but it requires a hell of a lot of organisation.

At both ends we needed: furniture, appliances, linen, toiletries and a fully decked out kitchen. Then there were items we carted back and forth each week: clothes, shoes, makeup, computer, personal items. I'm no Imelda Marcos – I own only a few pairs of shoes. Mark said many times, 'Make it easier on yourself and buy another few pairs.'

But my ingrained frugality doesn't allow me to spend

money on the same items, so I continue to transport two bags and a backpack (containing my office) twice a week. Oh, plus a bag for Mark, and two eskies with perishable and non-perishable food. Sometimes there's also a suit bag. It all adds up. The packing, watering plants, cleaning and shutdown / set-up on top of four-hours-a-week travelling, takes a full day out of the week. It's been testing for me. I have always found moving stressful. But there's nothing like a bit of boundary-pushing to know you're alive.

It is an exciting way to live with different walking tracks at each end. We get to let the lines go and cruise around Sydney Harbour at a moment's notice. Whenever we feel the boat rock as the wake of a ferry reaches us, we say, 'We're on a boat. We're on a boat,' to remind ourselves how lucky we are.

We got used to feeling 'at home' wherever we were and appreciated each place when we returned. I say, 'I love this place,' every time we go home to Newcastle. Every so often I have a meltdown, and then I fall in love with my life again. The only reason we paused was because of COVID-19. We took advantage of the break from the relentless travelling, and thankfully, we were both able to work productively from home.

Having the two places also made it convenient for others to stay with us when they needed accommodation in Sydney. One day in the first year of living in Sydney, as we were driving into the garage of the unit block, Mark said, 'Oh, I forgot to tell you that Steph's friend, Kayla, is going to be staying with us in a few weeks. She has a five-week physio placement for uni and asked if it was okay if she stayed.'

'When is this?' I asked apprehensively.

'Not next week but the week after.'

'Oh. We don't even know her.'

'I'm sure if it's Stephanie's friend, she'll be lovely.'

My brain was reeling. *I'll have no privacy. That's a long time for someone to be in the house. I hope she's easy-going. I won't get the peace and quiet I need to write. Argh.*

Mark sensed my discomfort. 'Is there a problem? I didn't think this would be a big deal.'

'Well, for me, it is.'

'There must be a reason.'

'I don't know. It's stressful for me to have people stay in the house.'

'It really is ridiculous.' He was starting to raise his voice. I had to find a way to explain.

'How many times in your life – I mean when you were a child, and with your own children – have you had people stay over at your place?'

'What do you mean?' Mark asked.

'I mean how many times have people – other than the people who live with you – slept at your home?'

'Seriously? I don't get what your point is. It would be thousands.'

'Yes. Exactly.' I paused to stop myself from crying. 'Well, I can't remember once. Not once.'

'Oh.' Mark sounded surprised.

'Until I was older, that is. But never as a child living with Mum and Dad, and hardly ever at all, really.'

'Mmmm. Well, that probably explains a bit.'

It is tough for me to recognise that my initial reaction

is always from fear. I immediately default to the worst-case scenario. Fight or flight kicks in whenever I feel threatened. *How am I going to relax in my own home? We're going to have no privacy.* The reality is that I never feel that way once visitors arrive. By then, I'm relaxed, and I love to entertain and socialise. It's the preparation, anticipation and attempting to get everything perfect that makes me anxious.

As it turned out, it was a pleasure to have Kayla stay with us. She ended up staying another four times over an eighteen-month period when she had physiotherapy placements in Sydney. We welcomed her each time and would have her back any time she needed a roof over her head. Once we moved to the boat, she enjoyed the novelty of it as she'd always been a country girl. It was lovely to see her excitement and know we were giving her a memorable experience. We call her our surrogate daughter now.

Stephanie ended up staying with us on the boat several times too, sometimes with Kayla. When they left, we missed their company. I enjoyed helping them out and cooking meals for them. It was good for me to have positive experiences of people staying over to conquer my old anxieties. It was also a great opportunity to get to know Stephanie better in a relaxed environment without the rest of the family. We got to know Steph's partner, Kyle, too, and whose company we enjoy. Early on, they accepted me, and now the four of us get together regularly, as we do with Josh and his partner Laila.

I still get overwhelmed when Mark springs new plans on me. My pre-programmed pattern, developed from years of anticipating the worst, automatically kicks in.

But now I take a deep breath to let my heart catch up to my overactive brain.

And then all is well.

Kayla came at the perfect time to help me live more freely in this area of my life.

21

SECRET DESIRES

We'd been planning a trip to Uluru for the official opening of Bruce Munro's Field of Light installation in 2016. All activities, events and meals were included in the four-day program, except for a gap on the Saturday afternoon.

Mark told me not to worry about booking anything as he'd arranged a surprise activity for us, but he wouldn't tell me what it was.

It wasn't unusual behaviour for Mark.

After lunch on that Saturday, Mark took me by the hand and led me through the doors of the reception area.

'Hi, I'm Colin, and I'll be your driver and pilot today.'

Colin had one of those thick English accents that sounded a bit Irish, but not quite. He slid the door of his van open, opened his palm and swept his hand in the air with the grace of a game show hostess, directing us in.

'Do you know what it is yet?' Mark asked.

The picture of the helicopter on the side of the van had kind of given it away. As we put our belts on, Mark rested his hand firmly on my thigh and took my fingers in his.

Before we'd left, I had researched the possibilities and had narrowed his surprise down to either a helicopter ride or a secluded romantic picnic. After intense questioning (What do I wear? How long will we be? Can I wear heels? Do I need sunscreen? Can I take a bag? Will there be a toilet?), he offered some suggestions. I decided on flat shoes and a long dress with a slightly outbackish print.

From the hints, I figured we weren't going skydiving, or riding Harley Davidsons or camels, which were the other possibilities.

We were driving through the gates to the helicopter when I asked how long we'd be.

'Oh, a while,' Colin replied. Typically, I asked to go to the bathroom before we left.

To keep our weight balanced, Mark sat in the front of the helicopter beside Colin, and I sat in the back with earmuffs on. I took slow deep breaths to calm myself as we lifted off the ground. I wanted to memorise every detail of this moment.

Occasionally, Colin talked to the base: 'We're commencing our reverse flight to Kata Tjuta and Uluru. Over.' But I was concentrating on the landscape. Every so often when I wasn't trying to spot camels or kangaroos, I would tap Mark on the shoulder, and he would turn around and smile or give me a thumbs-up. We couldn't speak privately as all three of us were connected by our mic and headphone sets. We hovered around the Olgas for a while, then Uluru. It was much wider than I'd imagined. All the pictures from the side make it seem long and skinny, but it was rounded from above with a point at one end. There was also more lush greenery around the base than I expected. It seemed enormous from the air – a huge rock sticking out in the middle of nowhere. The reds and browns changed colour from every angle.

'Because it's such a clear day, if you guys would like to, we can head a little further out to Mount Conner for a look at that too.'

'Sounds good,' Mark said.

I gave a thumbs-up. I'd expected expansive areas of deep orangey-brown soil, but I never imagined the outback to have so much vegetation – it was lush with plants and grasses. Trees and bushes clustered everywhere, and apart from a road every so often, there was not much else in sight. It was beautiful in its vastness. Sacred in its purity. Colin gave us a running commentary of interesting facts and the history of the area. It was another half an hour before we saw Mount Conner in the distance. I'd never heard of it. It looked similar to Uluru but had a completely flat top. Colin told us that people often mistake it for Uluru when they approach it as it's almost the same size.

'Because it is individually owned, we're able to land on the top of it. If you're feeling adventurous and would like to have a look around, the wind is being kind to us today.'

'Do you want to?' Mark turned, excited as a kid.

I shrugged. 'If you want to.' I knew he wouldn't pass up the opportunity.

'Why not?' Mark said to Colin.

As we turned and angled in, I wondered where we were going to land. It looked like the entire top was covered in trees and bushes. I felt butterflies again. Then a small T-shaped opening appeared. It seemed barely large enough to fit the helicopter. But Colin managed it perfectly.

Once we'd landed and disembarked, Colin grabbed a blue esky bag with water for us.

'We're currently over three hundred metres above the ground,' he said as he led the way.

We walked a few hundred metres, towards a break in the tree branches and dry bushes. I was frozen by the view in front of us. 'On top of the world' seemed like an understatement. But it was the sound that surprised me the most. The breeze seemed to echo, whooshing from far away. Ironically, the quietness was amplified, which made the silence loud. Eerie but beautiful. There was no-one anywhere near us. Except Colin. He helped Mark set up a table and two chairs that were tied to one of the trees near the edge. *People must do this a lot.* Even though it seemed as rare as a space expedition.

Colin began to walk backwards. 'I'll be back in an hour and fifteen. I have some paperwork to do. I know I don't need to say it, but please don't go too close to the edge. There are loose rocks, and the drop-off is severe.'

'Thanks, mate,' Mark said.

Colin disappeared into the bush.

My first thought was, *What the hell are we going to do here for that long?* My second thought was, *Mark wasn't that great at suggesting my attire for a rugged bush walk.* But when the esky turned out to contain a cheese platter, beer and a bottle of champagne, I realised there was more to the surprise.

Mark handed me a glass of champagne.

'It's taken a while to unravel my old life, but everything feels right and it's time to *attraversiamo,'* he said, speaking more quickly than he usually did.

He had memorised a line from Elizabeth Gilbert's *Eat Pray Love. Attraversiamo* means *to cross over.* We had watched the movie on the way over in the plane at my request. It was one of my favourite books. He guided me from the chair with both hands and knelt down on one knee. My lip started to quiver uncontrollably. I thought I had been so clever figuring out his surprise. The helicopter and the picnic – but I hadn't seen this coming.

A little black box appeared in his hand from who-knows-where, as he looked up into my eyes and said, 'Lisa O'Loughlin, I love you more than anything in the world, and I want to grow old with you.'

I swallowed hard.

'I want you to be my wife. Will you marry me?'

The sparkle of the ring caught my eye and tears began to well up. I couldn't steady my bottom lip. I hadn't allowed myself to think too much about getting married because there was a chance it may never happen for me. I was happy just to be with Mark forever, but I'd secretly hoped for this moment.

'So you haven't actually answered me yet.' Mark looked up into my watery eyes.

'Yes. Of course, yes.'

He put the ring on my finger and we tangled ourselves in a tight heart hug. I didn't want to let go.

'Does anyone else know?' I asked.

'Just your mum. I called her this morning to ask permission.' He read my curious expression. 'While you were reading by the pool.'

I was grateful that Mark had respected such a sacred moment between the two of us. I know Dad would have approved and appreciated how he'd asked Mum.

'I need to let the kids know before we tell anyone else.'

'Of course.'

'I just wanted it to be about us for tonight. You'll have to ring your mum though. She'll be waiting for your call. We can let everyone else know tomorrow.'

'By the way, how did you know I was going to say yes?'

Mark had a cheeky glint to his eye. 'I never ask a question if I don't know what the answer is going to be.'

How long had this been planned? When did he have time to organise the ring? Was this actually real? How could I not have known?

Unlike my first proposal sixteen years earlier – here, on the top of Mount Conner – I was in the right place. I didn't have a single doubt. As far as proposals go, Mark had pulled off a perfect one.

22

FUTURE FEARS

I had thrown an extra three garlic cloves in and was flipping the salmon with one hand while stirring the pot of parsnip puree with the other when my phone rang.

It was Mark's mum, Lyn. We chatted about ageing, and she mentioned that her daughter Kylie would likely be the one to look after her and Mark's dad – 'The girls usually do.'

'We'll all look after you,' I said. And then I added, 'I wonder who's going to look after me when I'm older.'

'Oow, wah,' Lyn said. It was long, drawn out and filled with fear. She was renowned for the phrase.

Lyn has three children and a flock of grandchildren. Some with partners too. She has plenty of people to choose from.

I've always been haunted by the fear of not having someone

to take care of me in the future.

Nanna used to say, 'You *have* to have children to look after you when you are old.' She would remind me of this almost every time I visited her. I've never wanted to betray my nanna's wise, old-fashioned advice, but life is not always that simple. Besides, I'd never have had children for this selfish reason alone. I wouldn't put that kind of pressure on any child.

I'd already come to terms with my decision not to have children, but Lyn caught me at a vulnerable ageing-future-thinker-with-no-children moment.

By now, the salmon was extra crispy skinned, and I wanted to get off the phone. Lyn told me not to worry about it, but secret tears that I'd long held in were close to sliding down the sides of my nose. As I hung up the phone, I tried to convince myself that I was just premenstrual.

Mark and I often joke about the things that are heavy on my heart, and him dying before me is one of them. I once asked if we could add a rule to our relationship – that we die at the same time. Or I go first.

'Considering you're seven years younger than me, that's probably unlikely,' Mark had laughed.

Even thinking about my life without him makes my stomach cramp.

I told him that when I die, I'm going to come back as a bird to annoy him. He always tells me not to worry about things that haven't happened and to enjoy all the time we do have. He reminds me to stay in the moment.

In my sturdier moments, I know that the future doesn't really exist. Anticipating what may happen is all in the imagination.

When the future arrives, it turns into the current moment again and can never be pinpointed or touched. The future is nothing but a story we create and believe. We can either dream up a happy future or fear a terrible one.

I've wondered if thinking about the future is simply anxiety. We all replay the same thoughts in our head over and over, day after day. They are so programmed in that we don't even realise they're on a loop. Imagine if instead of spending this time thinking about something that may never happen, we spent it on a project we've been putting off, or a way to contribute to people less fortunate?

I would love to think that Mark will be with me for every day I have left in this lifetime, but if that isn't how it works out, I will find a way to get through. Just like Mum has had to make her way without Dad. Just like so many who have shown how it's done before us. All that time wasted on worry is a distraction from living. I also believe that as twin flames, we have been connected previously and will be again – being apart would be only for a short time in the greater scheme of things anyway.

To counter my anxiety, I began to write down ten things I was grateful for everyday – all the blessings in my life. Gratitude works as an antidote to fear and reduces my anxiety. When I began to seek out positive moments to record in my gratitude journal, my focus changed. I appreciated beautiful moments and observed things I may not have otherwise noticed.

This is empowering, compared to the dread of life or fear of the future. The entries are a combination of silly, funny, serious and heartfelt impressions: morning cuddles from my husband, the scent wafting from my diffuser, how my plant bloomed its first flower or the friendly chat I had with the check-out operator at the local supermarket. I write down anything as long as it makes me feel good. Whenever I am feeling down, I flick through these pages. They contain thousands of tiny blessings that make me smile, change my mood and raise my vibrational energy. Gratitude helps us see the light on the dark days. My gratitude journals also act like a diary – an account of all the special memories I may never have remembered if I hadn't written them down.

Then COVID-19 arrived and thrust people all around the globe into unexpected solitude. We've been shown that whatever our individual circumstances are, they can change in a heartbeat. Our loved ones can leave us, or pass away, at any moment.

Even those who have kids may lose them tragically, negating the natural order of things. Others are estranged from their children. Having kids to 'look after' us when we are older is not only outdated; it's no longer practical. COVID-19 has taught us this. Even people with children weren't able to see them during the lockdowns. Many people with and without families died on their own. Our responsibility as humans is not to just procreate for the sake of tradition and because it's what our parents did. We have to consider the environmental impact. As we try to undo the damage done by our own and previous generations, it is our moral obligation to slow the population growth down to lessen the burden on our planet.

Our bodies are transitory, but our souls will live on.

It's natural that in this lifetime, we crave the connection of others, having all originated from one source. If we could get comfortable with being ourselves and on our own, much of our angst would fall away. We could let go of justifications, the need to prove ourselves and our obsession with seeking acceptance by others.

Whether we are in an intimate relationship or not, we need time alone – to breathe, contemplate our life and consider what our truth is as we travel our path. It's impossible to do so when we are consumed by the hustle and bustle of work, family and relationships.

I have stayed with my mum while she recovered from five operations in the past two years. Once I had to call the ambulance because she mixed her medications – I hate to imagine what would have happened if I wasn't there.

As I age, I'm not sure who will visit me, show me how to use the latest technology or help me get to places when I'm too old to drive; but I have faith that the Universe will look after me. The Universe has a greater plan, and whatever I am meant to go through, I will, no matter how much I resist or try to predict a future over which I have zero control.

Perhaps I'll never reach an age where I lose my independence. But if I do, someone I may have never met, someone who hasn't even arrived on this earth, will be there for me in ways I can't yet comprehend. Even if it's just to hold my hand, or visit me every other month, I need to trust that things are exactly the way they are meant to be.

I am slowly learning to trust in the now and appreciate every precious person who is here for me in this moment. The future will unfold naturally. *For* me.

I am opening my arms to meet it.

23

FINDING MY VOICE

Mum used to tell everyone that I still had the first dollar I'd ever earnt. My first experience in making money was in Year Six, when she gave me a handful of marbles in a green net bag. I played against the boys at recess and lunch. The originals were all different coloured cat's eyes; but after winning many games, I had an impressive collection of bonkers, pearls, steelys and swirleys. I carried them around in a clear Tupperware container, a mother hen protecting her eggs. At the end of the year, my attachment to the trend faded, and I sold my babies off for around twenty times the cost. I had a huge grin as I handed my money over the high counter to the bank teller, who stamped my *Star Wars* deposit book. *Cha-ching*. The more blue stamps, the better. As a young girl, I was taught the value of every dollar, and I wanted to save, not waste.

I've always spent my money carefully. I felt uneasy as I flipped open the thick, glossy magazine. I hadn't bought one since I was a teenager. I triple-checked how much it cost.

Gee, prices have gone up, I thought, ageing instantly – my grandparents said the same thing umpteen times. The magazine seemed a waste to me. The paper. The excessive number of ads. The gossip. Not interested.

But the glossy pages I was exploring didn't belong to your average trashy magazine. This was *Complete Wedding*. No-one else was home. I'd made a cup of tea and adjusted the cushions on my bed. Anyone watching would have thought I was about to conduct some sort of sacred ceremony.

It's a magazine, for goodness' sake. I couldn't help but laugh at myself. I'd only looked at a few pages when the voices flooded back. '*When's the big day? Have you picked your dress? Where are you having the wedding? Are you all organised?*' Argh. Every time I came across someone I hadn't seen for a while, they asked at least one of these questions. My responses were well rehearsed. '*I'm not sure. No, not yet. We haven't decided. We'll let you know as soon as we have a chance to talk about it – we've been really busy.*'

Was it normal that we'd been engaged for almost a year, and this was the first time I'd looked at a bridal magazine? Friends who got engaged after us had chosen a date, booked the venue, picked the dream dress and started arranging all the intricate details. My head started to spin. It wasn't a race, but I felt like the tortoise who'd fallen way behind. I needed to accept that I *was* engaged, and it *was* real. Time had passed. But it hadn't sunk in. Something else was holding me back.

'It's your day,' Mark kept saying. 'You've never been married, so it needs to be special. Think about what *you* want.'

I didn't know if I was the one making it hard. Was it that I had no idea where to start? Or was it that if I made a start, I'd feel pressured into finishing? The process would involve risks, decisions and, possibly, mistakes. Instead of brushing off my frustration and blaming my indecisiveness on my Libran star sign like I normally do, I searched for a reason for the way I was feeling – the honest reason. What seemed like an hour of examining the colour-filled pages had passed, and I nearly nodded off. Then all of a sudden, a light went on in my brain: I didn't actually know what I wanted. I didn't have an opinion. I didn't know what to do.

Our wedding was to be one of the only times in my life that I had to plan an event that was all about me. I wasn't used to making choices or doing what I wanted to do for no other reason than that I wanted to do it. Years before, when I was with Adrian, I'd felt ill after buying a pair of red patent-leather shoes – it was the first money I'd spent on myself in eighteen months. I clenched my teeth as I wrote one hundred and twenty-five dollars in that little book where I had to record every cent. I would need to think of a good reason to justify my extravagance.

Knowing what I wanted was a foreign concept.

Kids' parties, engagements, baby showers, weddings, birthdays – I was an expert guest, but an inexperienced guest of honour. Mark had organised a surprise thirty-eighth party for me and a wonderful fortieth; before that I hadn't starred at my own event since my Hansel and Gretel fifth birthday party.

Three decades had passed without all eyes being on me. As each birthday approached, the easy option was not to have a party – to let the occasions pass with a family dinner and no drama.

'But, Mum, everyone else is having a party.'

'You're not everyone else. You can have presents or a party. Not both.'

'Just be satisfied,' Dad would add.

If the focus was on me, I felt selfish and ungrateful. So yes, as I turned the pages of *Complete Wedding*, eloping crossed my mind. It was the economical and safe thing to do. Low fuss. It's what the *old* Lisa would have done. A big wedding day wasn't a necessity, and part of me thought it was absurd to indulge in such a way. If we eloped, it would be done. Finished. All over. We'd be married and the expectations would disappear.

But that's not what living life is all about.

The excitement would be over too, and I'd spent too long being a spectator in other people's lives while merely existing in mine.

In the same way that I've been known to hide important things in super-safe places that I always manage to forget, my inner desires and wants were buried. My voice too.

For many years, I sacrificed my own happiness to keep others happy. I was a pleaser – of others – not in relation to my own needs. This wasn't only about the wedding; I'd perfected this pattern over the years. I'd completed a Bachelor of Business Degree at uni, but I did it thoughtlessly with no end goal in mind. It was what was expected of me. I acted as if I'd been blindfolded, ready to pin the tail on the donkey of my career without too much conscious thought about where it landed. Without direction or vision, I majored in tourism and marketing. Not because I was interested in it, but because my friend Kristi was doing it. Where was that leader from the first day of kindergarten? Still stuck in the cubby house, most likely. I was incapable of making my own mind up, so I chose the easy way. Years frittered away in my relationships too; and I continued to sleep, eat and breathe the days away with no concept of how precious time was.

When I was asked in a writing workshop a few years ago to write about something I was *passionate* about, I froze. We only had ten minutes. I didn't want to look silly, but I didn't feel strongly about any cause or issue. Even if I found my voice, I didn't know what the hell it would say. One thing was for sure – it would be terribly croaky. I was never one to attend a picket line. What for? Human rights, abortion laws, asylum seeking? I didn't know enough about any of these topics to have a strong opinion. I hadn't been exposed to them. And in a way, I was grateful for that. As a child, I'd been protected from funerals, confrontation and the real issues of the world. Now this made me feel inferior because everyone except me seemed to have a special cause.

The ancient story of the Buddha, Prince Siddhartha, resonates strongly in my own life when I think about how I've been conditioned and protected from crucial life experiences. Prince Siddhartha's father desperately wanted to shield him from the suffering of life, and for him to never feel grief or misery, so he was kept locked away behind high palace walls in an environment of luxury. It had the opposite effect though. When Siddhartha finally left the protected grounds at twenty-nine years of age, he discovered the Four Encounters for the first time – old age, sickness, death and holiness. It was only then that he finally began his search for the meaning of life and renounced all earthly comforts. In trying to protect his son from suffering, the king inadvertently halted the spiritual development of his own child.

Protecting ourselves from pain simply delays the lessons we are bound to face. It prolongs rather than eliminate our suffering.

We will all face what we are destined to. In shielding children, we imagine we have control over them, but we don't. This thinking is scarcity and fear based. It isn't healthy.

But I was protected like that prince.

The result was that come elections, I'd vote for the party Dad voted for. When I began dating Mark, I voted the way he did because his reasoning made so much sense. But where was my own reasoning? I didn't get splinters from sitting on the fence but rather sore legs from jumping from one side to the other. As a result, I was easily manipulable. Only as I type this do I realise how many times unscrupulous people have taken advantage of me. Like a chameleon, I adapted easily to the environment around me, swiftly changing my colours to suit the needs and opinions of others.

The little girl in me was confident and self-assured, but somewhere on the way, I became scared to say what I thought. When I ponder on what I've accomplished in my life, I come up with a blank. How could I achieve anything of value when my voice was hijacked? Everyone says, 'Oh, but you came first at school, and you were a star student. You bought your own house.' So what? That was school. I don't want to live in the past, and I don't place significant self-worth on my monetary position. I want to achieve something of heartfelt value now – in my adult life. I want to rediscover my hidden voice.

As I paged through that bridal magazine, I heard Dad's booming voice ringing loudly in my ears, 'Good little girls should be seen and not heard.'

I have always feared upsetting people or saying the wrong thing. I've been told, 'You can't say that,' or 'Maybe you shouldn't have said that,' once too many times.

Growing up, I loved singing, but I never sang in front of the family. I'd sing in my head or wait until I was the only one home before turning the music up and pretend I was on stage. If Kim ever came into the room and heard me singing along to a cassette, my cheeks would turn pink.

She'd point and gasp. *'Ner ner ne ner ner.* I know your best vo-oice.'

No wonder it's been such a struggle to find my voice. It's been swallowed, restrained, muffled and shamed. It's no surprise I struggled to settle on what kind of wedding I wanted.

For my fortieth birthday party, Mark hired a singer as entertainment. At some point in the evening, I was called up to perform several songs. I was shy at first, but I took the mic.

My husband wanted to give me an opportunity to feel free to express myself and sing just because it felt good.

I'm no longer worrying about what my voice sounds like to others. I'm learning to let myself sing, at last.

Boho, elegant, beach, garden – what did I want? What was me? I truly had no idea.

But I was about to have an opinion, maybe for the first time ever.

24

UNPACKING MY CHILDHOOD

'Tell me more about your childhood.'

My writing mentor, Joanne, was distilling the core themes of my book during one of the early mentoring sessions. It seemed serendipitous not only that I'd met a published author at The Golden Door Health Retreat – the same place I'd met Mark – but that Mark had gently encouraged me to attend the talk in the first place. I believe that Nanna – having given me the money for the trip when I met Mark – was orchestrating all these chance meetings at my special place.

'It was all good,' I replied. 'We had no family dramas growing up. I actually had the perfect childhood. My family is amazing, and I feel lucky that I had such a great upbringing. I'm so appreciative of Mum and Dad, and apart from the obvious sibling fights, I got on pretty well with my sister. Since our mid-twenties, we have been closer than ever.'

She watched me intently as I spoke. 'You know that *no-one* has a perfect childhood,' she said.

'Yeah, true, but – there's really nothing out of the ordinary that sticks out.'

She was unconvinced.

Now she had me thinking on the spot. I felt the pressure building.

'There must be something you're blocking out or that's hard to face. Maybe you're just not seeing it.'

She seemed a little agitated. I suspected I'd been hard work for her – one of *those* women she'd talk about to her husband and say, 'I just don't know what to do with this one.' I had taken my sixteen thousand words on a writing retreat in Fiji, hoping she'd give me a tick of approval with plans to send me straight off to a publisher.

Now as she questioned me, I was concentrating so hard the sides of my forehead felt tight. She probed a little more.

'Is there nothing that stands out as…unusual?'

'Hmmm. Well, Mum is a bit OCD – obsessive compulsive. I mean, not officially. But it's pretty obvious. Everything was always in alphabetical order. She used to hang the clothes on the washing line with the same-coloured pegs and cut food up into exact cubes. There was even a 'reject' pile for the pieces that she couldn't avoid having triangular edges. But I'm sure that wouldn't be it.'

I laughed a little. Mum had always worn these habits as a badge of honour, and I had always thought of it as her thing.

My mentor got a look of sorrow and empathy in her eyes that I will never forget. She dropped her head into her fingertips. She seemed to be drawing all the information in. She didn't speak for a bit.

'I feel like you're skimming over this. Growing up with a mother with OCD can be a traumatic experience for a child. When you talk about her perfectionism and blah, blah, blah, it's not a joke. A child is, by nature, messy and is going to do things imperfectly and make mistakes – but if we're not allowed, then it affects who we become.'

I stopped laughing when I saw how serious she was. It was the first time I'd thought about it that way.

'I think this is a huge part of your backstory,' she suggested.

For months she had been telling me that I was skimming the surface in my writing and not going deep enough, that I wasn't getting to the core.

Sometimes as we move forward in life, we may as well be wearing a blindfold. We spin around, bumping into things, while repeating the same mistakes. It can be hard to comprehend what is blocking us from progressing because we keep looking at things from the same position. Our perspective becomes tainted by repetition. That's why the Japanese painter Hokusai painted hundreds of pictures of Mount Fuji from a variety of viewpoints. He claimed that we cannot know something until we observe it from multiple angles. That's why we need help – fresh eyes to look at our situation objectively from the outside in, instead of the inside out.

In this mentoring session, I was offered an outside view of my upbringing which became the catalyst to a process that got me digging deeper than I ever had before. I hadn't known this was a doorway to understanding myself better. It had nothing to do with my writing – she had taught me that the *craft* of writing is different from the *consciousness* that informs the writing. I was blocked because I needed to do more consciousness work.

'Anyone can learn how to write a plot and develop themes and character, but in memoir, you have to really learn and connect with yourself so you can connect with your readers. Who do you have to become to be an author?' she would ask.

I had assumed Mum's behaviour was 'normal.' I didn't know that other mums didn't choose the bread roll from the middle so it wasn't a hard end, or ask Baker's Delight for the lightest and softest loaf available. I didn't know that other mums didn't reject their kids clothing at the store cash register if the pattern didn't line up or it had a pull in the fabric. I didn't realise other kids weren't fastidious about avoiding getting dirt on their clothes for fear of upsetting their mums.

Until we know we have a problem, it doesn't exist. I had never thought about the implications; I had never known I needed to.

After the session, I paced for half an hour. I was on the boat, so I kept walking up and down the hallway. Ten steps turn, ten steps turn. The breeze blowing through from the front cabins was helping cleanse my thoughts. I needed to unwind. This couldn't be the thing that I'd been searching for, *could it?* How could something that gave my life structure and certainty have also been such a roadblock for me? My mentor's suggestion that my world may not have actually been so perfect or healthy was challenging to hear. I had difficulty letting it settle.

Mum's OCD had brought her positive attention. She was always the subject of jokes and was mocked by friends and family. Dad would laugh as he moved the cushions out of the way to sit on the lounge. 'Bloody cushions, I can't even live in my own home.'

'Your home looks like a display home,' visitors would proclaim. The compliments seemed to give her satisfaction and significance. She'd smile broadly, chuffed and proud. Her hard work always paid off.

All of our deepest beliefs and values are formed in our early years, so it was here when I learned that if things were untidy, they were icky and yucky. I neatened up anything that was out of place to keep Mum happy, not understanding why I was doing it. Kids copy. I dusted the leaves of the plants, cleaned up any mess, and kept the books and toys in pristine condition. Dog-eared pages in books were forbidden as was writing or highlighting in them. Mum had several changes of clothes for us so we were never seen in public with a tainted outfit.

Dishes never lasted long in the sink, and to this day, her bin is in the garage (at least fifteen steps away), not the kitchen. Her lounge is an L-shape, and she only ever sits on the end of the return – the part people put their feet on. She says it's to see the TV better, but Kim and I both know that her perfect display of ten cushions would be ruined if she were to snuggle comfortably into the corner.

Mum's rituals and need for order made her feel safe. She liked everything in its place. Maybe for her, it was a way of receiving the adulation she'd never been given as a child. She felt worthy when people noticed how good she was at something.

Without meaning to, Kim and I both adopted the same ridiculously high standards.

I loved playdough as a child, and now as an adult, I enjoy cooking when everything gets everywhere. But even as I relish making a mess and am in my element when things are chaotic and out of order, my unconscious programming kicks in to say, 'Tidy that up, and quickly.' I've trained for an entire lifetime to keep everything orderly because every time I made a mess as a kid, I got into trouble.

Mum was adamant that she didn't want to pass on her feelings of being unworthy to me and Kim. But sadly, she did just that. Every time she fixed something we didn't do perfectly, she unintentionally reinforced that we weren't good enough.

Mum used to vacuum the house – every day. Kim still mops the floors of her large house every day and hasn't stopped even though she often has pain in her wrists from continual housework. In my twenties, I used to clean for five hours each Saturday while Scott was at work. In my thirties, I still wanted the 'perfect home.' Not that many people got to enjoy it other than me and Adrian. My fastidiousness went further than just cleaning and spilled into rituals of double-checking and making sure everything was aligned and in order. I mastered perfect folds, hospital corners, made sure power points were off, and checked and re-checked doors were locked. Mum went one step further by putting red-coloured food in red containers.

I know now that this behaviour belies something much deeper, and being a perfectionist is not a badge of honour to wear pinned to your chest. At its heart, it is about the need to feel in control, safe and avoid being judged. These days, I'm much more relaxed. I don't think I have OCD. I ended up copying modelled behaviour without knowing anything different. I followed Mum's lead. Nowadays, Mark has fun mucking things up when he visits Mum's place. He purposely moves the glasses in the cupboard around so they aren't in height order, and pulls the spine of one book so it juts out in front of the rest. I know he is telling her in his playful way to chill out.

Having visitors over is stressful for someone with OCD traits. We are desperate for approval, for people to be impressed even as we prepare ourselves to be critiqued. Because if things aren't in order, then we're not in order. But it's a game with no winners. No-one actually cares. And with such high standards, the work is never done. It's relentless and tiring. It means there is always the next thing to fix, clean or sort. It's an endless distraction that keeps you from looking at yourself from another perspective – with compassion. I don't know how many times I've heard Mum and Kim say, 'I'm going to clean the cupboards out.'

It's an admission that things are not perfect as they are, but they will be. One day. *Who is looking in the cupboards anyway?*

The curse of the perfectionist is that we judge ourselves before anyone else has a chance to. *If I notice what's imperfect before anyone else does, then I'm off the hook. They'll know that my intention is to get it done. I know it's not perfect yet, but I'm working on it, and it will be soon.*

But it never will be. *It. Never. Will. Be.*

Whose life is ever really in complete order? It's hard for a perfectionist like myself to achieve our goals because nothing is ever perfect. And we wonder why we are always left feeling not good enough.

'We can get a cleaner in every second week to take the pressure off,' Mark offered on many occasions.

It seemed that as soon as the boat was clean, we'd go back to Newcastle and the house needed to be done. It was never-ending. Mark wasn't complaining. He just noticed how frustrated I was at not having enough time and was trying to solve the problem for me.

'It's all right. I can do it,' I'd say.

I resented how much time I needed to spend cleaning, but I'd feel like a failure if I couldn't do it all myself. I feared that people might say, 'She's not working full time and she can't even find the time to clean the house.' I felt the scrutiny, but it was self-directed, not from others. The fact was that we were living between two places and had two places to clean. We were juggling a gruelling lifestyle – I was writing a book, and one day a week was consumed with packing and being in transit. The weekends were filled weeks in advance, and I valued my leisure time more than spending it to keep up appearances. It wasn't until I was in my forties that we finally got a cleaner. Progress. Woohoo! (Although it was short-lived due to COVID-19.)

To keep everything in order, we can push life aside. Being super-organized, and cleaning endlessly, is a form of avoidance that keeps us from facing something. It's a distraction to keep us otherwise occupied. The joke in our family is that Mum wins the gold medal, Kim the silver and I am left with the bronze. It's not really funny though, because it's covering up deep pain.

We're all constantly searching for control, which doesn't exist.

These days I purposely allow things to remain a little untidy. I leave dishes in the sink and only clean when it's necessary. I'm no longer a compulsive cleaner. I want people to feel comfortable in my home. And I feel a sense of satisfaction that most of my books are riddled with highlighting and notes. It hasn't been easy to break my old patterns. Those ridiculous routines that I thought gave me control also stole the breath out of my life.

For so long, I was completely ignorant of what my own blockages were, though they'd been staring me in the face – like that Jesus statue at Nanna and Pop's.

To know yourself is to be curious.

To understand yourself is to listen to your inner voice and be open to fresh perspectives when they are offered.

To meet yourself is to be prepared to turn everything you believe is normal, upside down.

I thought I was always going to remain the way I was, that my habits were fixed and could never be unlearned. But then I realised I had the power to be whoever I wanted to be.

PART FOUR
Growing Up

25

TAKING RESPONSIBILITY

One uneventful Saturday afternoon when I was eleven, Dad asked me to help Mum with some housework and fold the washing for her.

'You can't make me,' I said.

'Don't speak to me with that tone, young lady.'

I squeezed my lips tight. *Whoopsy. It wasn't supposed to come out that way.*

'You'll do as you're told,' he said, aiming his pointer finger at my chest, the air whooshing out of his nostrils. 'Just remember, you're still a baby.'

'So when am I *not* a baby then?'

'Not until you're thirteen.' Dad's tone suggested that this milestone was way more than two years away. I didn't push him further, but when I became a teenager, it didn't surprise me that his rule had changed.

'You're still a baby until you're eighteen.'

Did he think I'd forgotten about our previous conversation?

Then at eighteen, the moving target stretched to twenty-one. Every time I reached an age, the goalpost seemed to creep further away. When I jokingly asked him whether I was still a baby in my mid-twenties, he winked at me and replied, 'You'll *always* be my baby.'

I made the mistake of thinking I knew everything when I was in my twenties. I'd blush and smirk if anyone ever said how smart, mature or grown up I was. It's a wonder I didn't start levitating – my ego was so inflated. My level of self-awareness had me believing that being the first in the family to go to university and a star student brought me status and significance. I couldn't help but be proud of myself. *What else could there be to learn?* Little Miss Me, in my first-ever relationship, working in my first full-time job, hadn't suffered through a break-up, hardship, or any real loss, grief or death. I hadn't even taken my first flight, but still, I genuinely thought I had life sorted out. I can chuckle now. I was far from worldly. We can only know as much as we have gone through at any one point.

In today's era of information overload, we can also be forgiven for convincing ourselves we understand life's experiences before we've lived through them. We skim the surface more broadly but have a deeper understanding of less. It doesn't matter how much we Google a topic; life teaches us what our devices cannot. Cognitive knowing isn't the same as 'real life' knowing. A person can read thousands of books, but unless the knowledge is put to good use, it's just a whole lot of stored information in the brain. We can read an inspiring quote and feel its resonance, but this doesn't mean we have felt – or experienced – the deeper meaning. There is usually a gap between where we want to be and how we are actually living our lives, between our superficial and deeper understanding of things.

Medical intuitive and author Caroline Myss explains how our bodies project an energy field which emanates from the positive and negative occurrences in our past. She believes our biography becomes our biology.

We draw on our stored emotions to help us make more informed decisions when we face similar situations in the future. If we haven't lived through an experience, our knowledge is superficial, not deep. Our wisdom isn't locked in until we feel real-life emotions and bear the consequences of our actions.

When we hear something that makes sense, we gain clarity in our minds, but it's only when we make a change that it becomes a pivotal moment in our lives. I've had many such moments of insight, but I've been too afraid to take action. These 'aha' moments didn't move me forward.

Until we embody our thoughts and words through experience, it doesn't become our reality. Our minds, bodies and spirits need to be aligned. We make changes when we integrate the mind, body and soul. We can't expect results if we focus all our attention on only one area. In the same way, a change in behaviour or habit doesn't work unless we shift our mindset or belief systems.

Dr Joe Dispenza, who is a leader in neuroscience, epigenetics and quantum physics, explains neuroplasticity: we can alter the pathways in our brains to change old patterns. In his *Rewired* series, he emphasises that our job is to go from knowledge, to experience, to wisdom. From mind, to body, to soul. From learning it with your head, applying it with your hands and knowing it by heart. Each human being has the potential to heal themselves and, in a sense, to become 'supernatural.' This occurs when our thoughts become more powerful than our bodies and environment.

That's why meditation and vision boards help create a desired future. I am beginning to realise that we all underestimate the power that lies within us. We default to old patterns when we haven't healed the connection to our past. When we have healed, the old pathways aren't our backstop anymore.

* * *

A couple of years ago, I was co-facilitating a Midlife Memoir writing seminar when my writing mentor said, 'You don't grow up until you take complete responsibility for your own life and stop blaming others. Until then, you are still a child.'

On hearing her words, I felt as if a golf ball had lodged in my throat. *Had I really grown up yet?* I was in my forties, for goodness' sake. But had I accepted full responsibility for *everything*? In that moment, I was humbled. Could I accept that any ongoing discomfort in my life was because of my own choices and reactions?

I was taken aback when I first heard that she wasn't keen on mentoring young writers. She prefers to work with women over forty-five who, in her words, 'have suffered enough and have enough perspective on life.' I was forty-two when I went on her writing retreat in Fiji and felt like the junior of the group. I'd always been labelled mature, so I assumed I was a grown-up. But after the Midlife Memoir workshop, I wasn't so sure. Many of us go through life blaming our upbringing, parents, partners – anyone but ourselves. We'd rather clutch onto our long-held beliefs (formed before we knew enough to understand), and be right, rather than free.

In James Hollis's book, *The Middle Passage: From Misery to Meaning in Midlife*, he identifies three stages in life characterised by different kinds of thinking. Childhood is a time of magical thinking, where we act as if no dream is impossible. In adulthood we engage in heroic thinking, where we become more realistic but also still hope to accomplish our goals. The middle passage is when realistic thinking sets in, tempered with perspective.

First, we are dreamers, then we are warriors wanting to conquer the world, then in midlife we have a chance to reflect and evolve with greater self-awareness. We become more interested in ourselves and the meaning of our lives instead of worrying about keeping up with everyone else's.

Society instils the belief that we are old enough to start driving when we're sixteen, and can vote and drink alcohol when we turn eighteen. Typically, we are told we become grown-ups in our twenties. In reality, this is probably more of an exception than a rule. 'Grown-up' is a title to be revered and is often thrown around earlier than earned (I don't think that's why my dad kept shifting the goalposts – he was just suiting himself).

Of course, we can learn from people of all ages, including adolescents, the elderly, and especially children who show us in their free-spirited way, how to behave and view the world detached from ego.

The dear, close friends I used to work with are all different ages ranging from thirties to sixties. When we met, we were all in the preceding decade. We all connect and bring different skills to our friendships. No-one acts superior or exudes an 'I've got this sorted' attitude. We all respect every age, knowing each of us has something unique to offer. The younger ones share fresh ideas and modern perspectives while the older ones offer wise advice and stories from life events and challenges. We need connection with younger people so we don't lose touch with the next generation, and older people so we appreciate where we've come from.

Best-selling author Elizabeth Gilbert made me laugh out loud once on a Rachel Hollis RISE podcast episode (Reclaiming Your Power) when she recounted how a young woman stood up at one of her presentations to ask a question. When she said that she was twenty-one, Elizabeth Gilbert interjected, 'Oh sweetie, I'm sorry. I'm sorry, but it's going to get so much better. I had to be twenty-one once too. But you'll get through it, and someday you're going to be fifty and it's going to be awesome.'

We never get to an age where we've learnt it all. We are constantly becoming who we are meant to be – right up until the day we die. We also let go of being right and become more curious about possibilities and alternative options as we get older.

Who would you spend an hour with on this seat if you could choose anyone, with no limitations? asks a social media post with an empty park bench.

I'm always interested to read people's comments. The millennials (or younger generations) often choose an influencer, celebrity or sporting personality. Older folk tend to choose a parent, grandparent or a loved one who has passed, to spend one more hour with them. When we are younger, we don't seem to appreciate the generations that have come before us. We are too busy in the heroic phase, trying to make our mark on the world.

We so desperately want to be grown-ups, but we want to earn the title the easy way. We think that when enough years have flipped over on the calendar, we are mature. But there is more to growing up than accumulating birthdays.

I finally reached a place where I could challenge my conditioning. And I realised that growing up wasn't based on a number.

26

LIFE HAPPENS FOR ME

Mark and I hired a boat on the Canal du Midi in Southern France in 2015. On Bastille Day, we tied it on several bollards and went for a walk to check out the festivities. I felt bile-rising-in-my-throat sick when we returned and saw the curtain behind the door flapping in the breeze.

'Shit. You stay there,' Mark said, going ahead of me.

The window on the port side had been removed. All the devices and electrical items that Mark had been charging were gone. Thankfully, I had put a few valuable items in the safe, and I had our passports in my handbag, but everything else had been rifled through.

I wasn't shaken so much by the objects that had been taken, though thousands of dollars' worth had been stolen: handbags, backpacks, iPads, hard drives, headphones, toiletries and cash. It was knowing that a stranger had touched all our belongings. I felt violated. My backpack had even been used as the getaway bag.

I lost my appetite that night.

'I hope they can't access all of our personal details.'

'Don't worry, babe. It's only stuff. I've notified Apple that the iPad has been stolen.' Mark hugged me. 'I'm more upset about the hours I spent downloading movies for us to watch when we don't have wi-fi.'

I went to bed that night with my handbag containing our important documents at the foot of the bed under the sheets. Mark spooned me, which helped calm my shaking body.

We now call it 'Bas-steal-day.' It was awful, but this experience changed my life in ways I couldn't have predicted. Of course, it cemented the unimportance of material things. And we were lucky – we hadn't been physically hurt. But most importantly, on that day, I stopped worrying about being robbed ever again because it had already happened. It made me appreciate that when we spend time thinking 'what if this' or 'what if that' happens, we're wasting time in the present moment. If we are going to be robbed, we will be. Worrying about it is not going to stop it from happening. If we added up all the time we spent worrying and ruminating, we would be shocked at how much we squandered instead of investing it in productive and worthwhile ventures.

In the past, when I was going through troubled times, I had cried, *'Why is this happening?'* or *'I can't believe this is happening to me.'* Now I understand that is a victimized mindset. But I am no longer playing that game with myself or the Universe.

Now, when things happen, I choose to see it has happened *for* me rather than *to* me.

Over time, I've begun to recognise that everything in my life has happened *for* me.

I'm not diminishing the impact of terrible events, nor am I suggesting we attract them or are in any way to blame for them. But at some point, we need to deal with – and heal – these wounds. We cannot undo the past, and it's a waste of time attempting to try.

I'm not referring to severe trauma (rape, war, violence or abuse), but to the everyday traumas or 'little t's' that every single one of us encounters at some time, such as the hardships in relationships, our hurt feelings, past resentments and limiting beliefs. These are life events we can overcome and use for the greater good of humanity if we do the work to understand why they have occurred in our lives and what we have learned from them.

If we continue to suffer because of these types of incidents, we may want to ask ourselves if we are choosing to continue to suffer. This is what the Buddhists refer to as the second arrow. There is always pain in life, but we don't have to suffer over our suffering too. We are always faced with trials. That is what life is about. These are obstacles we must work through to get to the next season of our lives. They give us emotional muscle, the wherewithal to change the trajectory of our path and provide us with invaluable knowledge to use in the future or pay it forward to others. We can all surely cite examples of a time of hardship turning into a blessing in disguise.

Benjamin Hardy, best-selling author and organisational

psychologist, talks about post traumatic gain. Instead of focusing on the negative consequences of our traumas, his research concludes that we can be better off as a result of trauma. It allows us to be more capable if we find the value in our experiences.

When I first started writing this book, I heard about Joseph Campbell's 'hero's journey' which describes the arc of human transformation. The protagonist is called to an adventure. Once she ventures forth, she will have to overcome trials and obstacles, including her own worst fears. When the protagonist returns to the ordinary world, having gained a tangible or emotional treasure, she is changed, in some way, for the better or worse. She has outgrown her old life and finds some kind of resolution in a new state of normal.

We each repeat the process over and over, and this is how we continue to evolve.

We are each the heroes of our own stories – either intentionally or by accident – and the process of evolution is a painful one. We are invited to be brave so we can contribute to humanity. What we learn helps us face our fears and motivates us to do hard things for the greater good.

We all face different obstacles. What scars one person may be minor or barely visible in another. You may be unscathed after a robbery, for example, but when I was robbed, it shook me to my core.

My failed relationships with Adrian and Scott helped me to know with certainty when my 'forever person' arrived in my life. Difficult people came into my life to teach me resilience and to ignore the voices outside. My anxiety has given me the chance to develop a heightened awareness of my breath and to learn that I am the one in control of my own thoughts and body.

If enough time passes, we can look back on most situations where we have suffered and see that it was a precursor for enlightenment or instigated an insight to guide us through a future hurdle. We cannot always find the deeper meaning as events are unfolding, but over time, we become more proficient in finding it and in quickening our recovery.

We all get to 'slay the dragon,' as Joseph Campbell's journey suggests. Metaphorically speaking, it is the moment we disconnect from our egos, which can be the biggest threat to our transformation. I had always possessed a trusty dragon-slaying sword, even though I had to travel thousands of miles looking for it elsewhere. Dorothy, too, went adventuring on the yellow brick road in the movie, *The Wizard of Oz* and faced The Wicked Witch of the West several times on the way. She didn't realise that the ruby slippers she wore the whole time could have taken her home at any point.

All I needed to do was slay that part of myself. I had to do what scared me. Run *to*, not *from*. We often look for answers from others, but they are always within ourselves – closer than we imagine. Focusing on what is happening in other people's lives and caring what anyone else thinks distract us from our own development. It's hard to admit to not-so-admirable traits within. The 'evil' we see in others actually reflects our own insecurities – it's our shadow.

I needed to love my dragon, the part of me I didn't love, even though I thought I did. When we love our dragon, we expand the knowingness of self. Every journey we go on asks us to give something back to life. I had always been fighting myself. My exes and the difficult people in my life weren't my antagonists: I was. When we blame other people, we convince ourselves that they are the problem. We pretend that we are right, and they are wrong. But ultimately, we are responsible for our own happiness. The blame we place on others, and the negative emotions that go with this, end up being poisonous – to us.

Whenever I have been frustrated or unsettled, it wasn't anybody else's fault. Others have only been mirrors reflecting my own shortcomings back to me. They highlighted that my problems were within me, as were the solutions.

Can we avoid our dragon altogether and never get anything wrong so we never have to go looking for our swords? It's doubtful, and why would we want to? Rachel Hollis – New York Times best-selling American author, motivational speaker and new age influencer / blogger – goes as far as saying, 'I hope you fail.'

In failing, we learn to fall, and then we stand back up again. This is how we can encourage each other, by having meaningful discussions when we make mistakes instead of feeling ashamed and guarding ourselves from acknowledging our humanness. If everything went smoothly, how dull would our lives be? We wouldn't have the dark to appreciate how radiant the light is. We wouldn't be transforming into the person we are here to be. We would be stagnant – not to mention boring. Imagine watching a movie of your life where there is no low point, turning point, villain or moment where your adversity grows into your superpower.

One beautiful and generous woman – Ali – in my writing tribe is a survivor of breast cancer who spends much of her time helping empower other women with her self-love message. She has endured firsthand the result of toxic thoughts and holding on to emotions. In the beginning, I'm sure she would have thought breast cancer was happening *to* her, but she says now that it happened *for* her. Having been through the terrible experience and come out the other side, she is a source of strength and support to other women experiencing the same challenge. It is her mission to encourage all women to love and care for themselves, and shift from surviving to thriving. She also believes that everything good in our lives comes from loving ourselves. She is an example of an Earth Angel who needed to be brave, a survivor and live out her intended purpose. She couldn't have done so without having lived this. Before cancer, she wouldn't have had the motivation, courage or personal experience to take on the inspirational work she is doing.

Only when we conquer our fears and realise their origin do we go beyond being affected by them and regain our power. Our current problems reawaken longstanding issues from our childhoods and bring them back into our consciousness. Without this awareness, we can struggle for years thinking we have bad luck, or the world is against us. This is all part of the process too. When our internal war reaches a tipping point, we know it's time to take the next step in our development. We are only rewarded after the struggle.

I know the butterfly analogy is overused, but I feel a little like I've been incubating in the chrysalis and waiting to be a butterfly for far too long. My limiting beliefs have had the same effect as the chrysalis being wrapped tight, making it that bit harder for the butterfly in me to push through. As soon as I loved and accepted myself, I stopped being at war. The war I'd been blaming on others was my own.

'This too shall pass,' (as Wayne Dyer and many others have said) and when it does, you have to look for the learning buried in the suffering. The pain is *for* us. Instead of asking, 'Why me?', I have learned to say, 'Thank you for the lessons I am about to learn from this hardship.' In the midst of the tough times in my life, I have come to trust that the blessing in the darkness will come.

For most of my life, my worst fear was that one of my parents would die.

But isn't it an inevitable (even blessed) part of life for a parent to die before us? Having lived through and survived my dad's passing, I now view his death as something that happened for me. It prompted me to stop procrastinating with the most valuable resource – time. It was the devastating wake-up call that changed my life. It was my *call to action*. If Dad hadn't passed away when he did, I may have kept repeating the same pattern over and over, and got to the end of my life having wasted the whole damn thing.

Out of all the darkness came a light that may have never presented itself otherwise.

I hope he knew as he left this world, that I was ready to embrace it.

27

NO GETTING BETTER

'Will it get better?' I asked when I broke my nose jumping back and forth between my bed and Kim's when I was five, and whenever I fell off my bike and scraped my knees, or when over two hundred chicken pox covered every (yes, every) inch of my body when I was fourteen. I must have asked this question hundreds of times as a kid. Every scratch, bite or imperfection was a reason to beg Mum and Dad to reassure me that I would get back to my old self.

I was used to Mum's reply. 'Yes, of course, it will. Stop worrying.'

Dad provided the tough love and usually said something like, 'You'll be fine. Stop being such a baby.'

They were always proven right. Breaks, bruises, cuts and

blemishes always healed.

But in 2016, I noticed changes to my hearing. I thought I was going deaf when certain sounds became muffled. But I was only forty-one. It didn't make sense.

'I'm sorry, I didn't quite hear you,' I'd say, and I tried extra hard the second time someone spoke. Sometimes I'd pretend that I'd heard instead of asking for a third repeat.

It was confusing because at the same time, I was also super-sensitive to certain noises. Loud bangs startled me more than they should have, and the TV always seemed too loud. I ignored it for a while, but I sensed Mark becoming frustrated that I couldn't hear everything he was saying.

It began the previous year when Mark, Stephanie, Josh and I were in the car together, travelling from the airport after a flight from Melbourne.

'Whoa!' My head jolted back into the headrest.

'I heard that,' Stephanie said from the backseat.

'Seriously? Did you hear it too?' I asked Josh as I turned my head to face him.

'I did, actually,' he said with a surprised expression.

'What *was* that?' Mark said.

'Who knows. Maybe my eardrum just burst. How weird. I felt a loud crackle when I yawned. Like an explosion. It seems to be okay now.' I had been trying to equalise and clear my blocked ears after the flight.

Had that noise in the car been something sinister?

I booked an appointment with an ear, nose and throat specialist. She did some hearing tests, and I agreed to try grommets – ear ventilation tubes – to help my ears to equalise while flying.

'I can't stand it if it's like this forever. It's like a constant ringing. I don't know what to do,' I said to Mark when I returned to the boat after being in hospital.

My breathing was shallow and short.

'I'm sure it will settle down. Give it some time. Call the doctor if it's really worrying you,' he reassured.

Everything was loud. I felt claustrophobic. The noises around me had changed, and this was sending me into a panic. Everything sounded like horses stampeding towards me. My heart kept racing. I waved my fingertips in front of my face and swallowed with difficulty. I had a newfound empathy for anyone who was deaf or had a hearing impediment. I hoped I wasn't being punished for those stupid games at school where I always chose being deaf over being blind when asked which I would prefer.

After a week or so, the noise settled down. Perhaps I had just become used to it. I had to wear earplugs for a while if I went to a loud venue or anywhere with lots of background noise. Friends would say, 'You'll have to speak up. I can't hear you,' when I felt as though I was yelling at the top of my voice.

On the positive side, flying was more pleasant. The air had a hole to escape through, and there was no build-up of pressure. My follow-up hearing tests were pretty much identical, so the problem hadn't been solved, only my ability to auto-equalise. The grommets would last twelve to eighteen months. Permanent grommets leave the eardrum irreversibly scarred and that wasn't a sacrifice I was going to make. My hearing was literally off the chart (way above normal) in some frequencies, and there needed to be an explanation for the weird sensations which I still feel to this day.

I went to see an ear, nose and throat surgeon to see if he could help me. Weirdly, he did some tests on my eyes. I trusted he knew what he was doing. Afterwards, he sat me down and pushed a piece of A4 paper towards me with three words on it.

'I think you have SCD.'

What the eff?

'Superior canal dehiscence.'

When he explained further, it seemed more inferior than superior, but all the symptoms I'd been experiencing made sense.

'Some people are born with a fragile bone between their inner ear and their brain. A small impact can cause this bone to break. It distorts hearing so all of your internal sounds become much louder, and you can hear certain frequencies at higher-than-normal levels. I need to send you to a specialist. She will do a VEMP [vestibular evoked myogenic potential] test to confirm the diagnosis for you.'

Another specialist. She must be a really special one.

'I see that you have a tendency to panic a bit regarding this. It's okay. Sometimes just knowing that this is what it is seems to help. Some people think they are going crazy with all these weird noises in their heads,' the doctor told me.

Not long after, the *special* specialist confirmed SCD after a series of tests that measured how my muscles and eyes responded to stimuli.

It made sense that I couldn't hear certain sounds that I should have been able to, and that I could also hear things that I wasn't supposed to be able to. It was like I had supersonic hearing – that was how she described it.

'When I have to tell kids they have this condition, I tell them they'll make a great detective one day. It's quite rare. I've only ever seen a few hundred cases.'

'Can it get better?' I asked.

'Unfortunately, not.'

I must have heard her incorrectly. Everything gets better, doesn't it?

Not in this instance.

When Mark came home, I was excited that after more than a year, I had an answer.

'At least you know what it is. Is there a cure, or can they do anything about it?'

'There's an operation, but the condition itself has only recently been discovered, and there's a risk I could go completely deaf so I'm not doing that.'

'They may be able to do something in the future,' he said.

This was the first time I had a health issue that was permanent. It couldn't be fixed with healthy eating or natural remedies. I had to deal with it.

'Now I know why I'm always the last one to finish eating.'

'I thought it was because you talk so much,' Mark smiled.

'Ha-ha. You're too funny. I really can't hear people talking, or the TV, while I'm chewing. I didn't even realise that I had to stop chewing so often.'

Mark also has a low voice, which is a harder frequency for me to tune into easily.

I was pleased to know that I wasn't going deaf, but my symptoms were here to stay.

When I blow my nose, it sends me dizzy and way off balance. Sometimes I sway thirty centimetres to one side if I'm standing. The galloping horses, I discovered, was the amplified sound of my heartbeat. I hear an intense grating noise when I brush my hair under the hairdryer. This explains why I feel so anxious sometimes. I need to relieve my ears with a cotton bud nearly every day – they feel itchy all the time. I want the feeling of water being trapped in my ears to flow out like it did after a day at the beach as a kid. But it never does. When I'm on the road and there are altitude changes (which is more often than you can imagine), I feel like I'm on a plane descending. After plane trips, I find myself saying, 'Sorry, I didn't hear you,' for a week afterwards, sometimes longer. I have intermittent ringing, and sometimes one ear becomes muffled for a minute or so. When I'm meditating and do slow expanding breaths, I clearly hear my bones clicking into place in my neck and back. Every single breath. The strangest sensation of all is that when it's quiet, I hear a distinct fluttering each time I blink. I literally hear the sound of my eyelids dragging over the ball of my eye. If I think about it too much, it freaks me out, so I'll stop there.

When something changes, we long for life to go back to the way it was before. Why do we fantasise about the times that were, instead of being inside the time that is here?

'Christmas isn't the same as when we were kids.' No shit, Sherlock. When we were young, our objective was to have a great time. That's when we were innocent and defining events hadn't happened, and we got to unwrap presents instead of unpacking our lives. It was before the family break-ups, feuds and deaths. We can't go back, but we know more now and can change how we go forward.

Perfectionists always want to go back before the mistake we made that ruined our lives. But shit happens to all of us, so we need to get friendly with the discomfort of the moment because it's all we have.

When I got this diagnosis, I searched for meaning. My body once again was talking to me – this time, my ears were inviting me to go inwards for the first time in my life, to stop listening to all the voices around me and worrying about everything happening to others. This was a hint from the Universe. Why else would the sounds inside me be amplified and those outside be dulled? Metaphorically, I was being guided to listen to what *my* body was saying. I was being forced inwards, instead of outwards. I needed to listen to my own thoughts instead of following others.

I was intrigued that all this was happening at the exact time I was delving deep within to write this book.

It's ironic that I complain like a hypochondriac about temporary pain – a sore wrist or a cut on my finger – but I don't complain much about my ears even though it affects me daily. I know the condition is never going to get better. No-one can say or do anything to reassure me. There is no answer, only acceptance.

'It is what it is,' as Mark says.

I stopped focusing on outside noises when I knew there was no solution. I kept my thoughts to myself. Otherwise, I'd constantly be whinging, and what would be the point of that? Instead, I've found positive meaning in this situation. Each day, I send myself healing energy and hope for a miracle cure or future advances in technology. But I don't waste too much time there.

It was a ridiculous coincidence that through my writing mentor, I met the author Graeme Freidman, whose most recent novel, *What the Boy Hears When the Girl Dreams*, is about a boy who has SCD and hearing superpowers. Graeme had heard about the condition and researched it because he was fascinated by its peculiarity and thought it would make an interesting story. After we met, he asked me to read the book and offer him some insights and feedback.

Everything becomes aligned when you are in the flow.

As children, we are told over and over that things will get better, so we come to believe this as a truth. But sometimes they may not. Some relationships will end. Ageing leads to changes in the body that cannot be reversed. No amount of time passed will heal some wounds, both emotional and physical.

To hope for things to get better means to want to switch things back to the way they were. We have to be content with being in the present. 'Will it get better?' keeps us in the past.

All we can do is focus on the relationships we have and remain rooted in our appreciation for what we have right now.

28

THE FAMILY TREE

As kids, Kim and I had many fun times playing on Nanna and Pop's beanbag. We'd jump on it and punch it into a comfy position. Sometimes we'd take turns, and other times, we'd say, 'One, two three,' and sit down at exactly the same time so one of us wasn't higher than the other.

One day I unzipped it, curious about what was inside. When thousands of tiny white spheres spilled out like volcano lava, the blood whooshed to my face.

'I didn't mean to –'

'You'd better pick up every one of those,' Nanna said with pursed lips.

I had to fix my mistake by scooping beans up and putting them back inside the bag. They were charged with static electricity and stuck to my hands, the floor and the furniture. It took ages to clean up. But Kim helped me.

My curiosity about how things worked compelled me to explore what made the bag mouldable. But in that moment, an inadvertent trauma set in: my brain linked being inquisitive with punishment, reinforcing the same terror and shame I felt when I had turned Mrs Forster's speaker on in Year Two. I became wired with a fear response without being aware of it.

As a result of the beanbag incident, I become less curious and more obsessive about never making a mess.

It was not a significant trauma in the scheme of things. But it altered my perception of the world and my behaviour forever after. I also downplayed it, and thousands of similar moments, to avoid getting into trouble.

Most of us carry experiences through our lives that trigger fear responses. Post-traumatic stress disorder (PTSD) is usually attributed to survivors of violence, abuse, genocide or war. But trauma can result from seemingly innocuous experiences. The pain of an experience can cause us to change our response when we face a similar situation again. If we're bitten by a dog as a child, we often come to fear all dogs.

If we don't deal with our own trauma, we take on negative patterns of behaviour and unleash a lifetime of suffering. Because it doesn't rank as a serious trauma, we often struggle to make the connections. For far too long, I couldn't understand why I was so fearful. Why had I always been an extreme perfectionist? Why so often in my life had I felt anxious and claustrophobic?

When I first heard about the concept of intergenerational trauma and family constellations, I wanted to investigate further. I wanted to know how unresolved trauma could be passed down through the generations without each person experiencing the traumatic event firsthand.

This led me to the work of Bruce Lipton, a renowned cell biologist who has worked extensively in the area of epigenetics – the study of how your behaviours and environment can cause reversible change that affect the way your genes work without altering your DNA sequence. Dr Lipton says the environment we are exposed to can affect our cells more than our DNA. I found it fascinating how human cells adapt after a trauma experience and that these changed cells live on in future generations. It's as if the cells are on alert, scarred by the events of the past, protecting themselves from future threats that haven't happened.

It sounded like a way to blame the previous generation for our wounds. But it seems as if one person in a family takes on the role of the *finder-outerer*. Despite the beanbag setback, I am that person. I've always been the inquisitive soul who needed to explore all the whys. I began to research my family tree.

Fascinating facts and patterns began popping up like precious new seedlings breaking through the soil. The book, *It Didn't Start with You,* by Mark Wolynn revealed to me how we have core language relating to our greatest fears, and that sometimes we use words that are uncharacteristic – not our own. I considered some of the phrases I regularly repeated to myself: 'I won't be able to breathe,' and 'I don't want to be left in the gutter.' The first rings true because of my anxiety and claustrophobia, but the second contradicts my belief in trusting the Universe and being able to look after myself.

Wolynn cites many examples in the book, of people who suffered for decades with debilitating fears, which could be traced back to the unresolved pain of previous generations. Sometimes knowing that it wasn't their pain was enough to free these sufferers; for others, more work and therapy were required. Offspring of Holocaust victims, in particular, are severely affected by their ancestors' experiences. Much research confirms that the children and grandchildren of survivors suffer severe trauma and PTSD, even though they never experienced the event firsthand.

According to Wolynn, we share a cellular environment with our family before we are even conceived. The ovum we each come from is already in our mother's ovaries when our grandmothers are in the later stages of pregnancy with our mother. All three generations – grandmother, mother and early traces of ourselves – are inside the same body and environment for a period of time. If our grandmother faced trauma during her pregnancy with our mother, we could be harbouring the suffering inside us and reacting to the emotions that were felt two generations ago.

It seems to be widely accepted, from the reading I have done, that trauma can leave a chemical mark on one's genes which, in turn, can be passed down.

I read several books and did my own investigations before interviewing Mum and Dad's sister, Aunty Linda, hoping to collect three generations' worth of information from both sides of the family.

When I asked Mum who in the family was 'in the gutter,' or was afraid of 'ending up in the gutter,' she said her grandfather

Norris (my great-grandfather) was 'a bit of a lad' and would end up rolling drunk in the gutter. This didn't quite seem to fit, but something else she told me, did. As an only child, Mum was in charge of her parent's finances when she was in her fifties, and my nanna in her seventies. Nanna often said to her in relation to pension funds running low, 'What – are you going to leave me in the gutter?' On hearing this, I felt myself release the quicksilver shiver of fear I had whenever I talked about being in the gutter.

I scribbled a family tree in my notebook and added snippets of information as I received them. I filled the page quickly, and it sure led somewhere I wasn't expecting.

Among my grandparents' and great-grandparents' generations, there were ten instances where someone lost a child. The children were all different ages and died from varied causes. Many had cancer or other illnesses, one died after an epileptic fit in the bath, one was a twin that died at birth, another perished in a car accident. I almost dropped the pen when I connected the pieces.

Could those early misgivings of mine about bringing a child into the world be my ancestors' fears, not mine? Did I inherit an intense concentration of loss from the twenty parents before me who had outlived their children? Could these fears have travelled through my bloodline to reach me, warning me of the pain they'd experienced and their devastation and regret for the children they were supposed to protect? No wonder I'd harboured a sense of dread when I thought about bringing a child into the world.

Was intergenerational trauma the explanation for those words I'd written in my journal all those years ago? *How could*

I bring a tiny human into this scary and unpredictable world of chaos and disorder? How could I possibly be responsible for and protect a precious life when so much could go wrong?

I had expressed their fears in my own words. Those words didn't ring true for me at the time. As I realised I'd written them before I knew this information, I felt a tingling sensation down my back. *Could this just be a coincidence?*

There was more. My great-grandfather (on Mum's side) and my grandfather (on Dad's side) served in the first and second World War respectively. My great-grandfather served in the First Machine Gun Company and was one of the last Gallipoli veterans. Pop was a gunner and served in Borneo and Papua New Guinea. Pop used to tell me about the conditions of being in the trenches and underground in confined spaces. Could this have contributed to my fear of not being able to breathe? As a child, I'd been stuck in a lift and a fire stairwell, experiences which only compounded this trapped feeling. Mum told me she had been traumatised when her grandfather left her alone a couple of times as a four-year-old while he went to the pub.

In that era, children did die more frequently, and men did go to war. Nevertheless, when I related these incidents to my own life and linked the pieces, I felt illuminated with understanding and compassion — both for my own fears and for my ancestors' suffering. According to Wolynn, we don't necessarily need to know all the details. Sometimes it's enough for us to identify the connections. It was comforting to discover that my worries, fears, anxieties and unnatural fears of the world may not all be mine.

Wolynn goes on to show that adoption in previous generations can result in abandonment issues in subsequent generations – feelings of being unloved, without good reason. I wondered if this explained some of Adrian's defensiveness as he was adopted. Abuse may cause fear and a feeling of waiting for bad things to happen. When genes carry defensive energy, it may be more difficult for us to learn to trust people.

I highlighted much of the text in Wolynn's book. He explained how sometimes people don't want to be cured. Being a victim can serve us in some way, so we seek out and create circumstances to attract abandonment scenarios in our lives to reinforce that we are *right*. This is how we stay trapped in our dramatic stories. A supportive partner will stick around, but sometimes after decades of attempts to help their spouse, they have no other choice but to give up – for their own sanity and fulfillment. We often need therapy later in life to remove all the layers around us that are sourced in other people's issues.

Wolynn explains that when a child disassociates from parents, they are not erasing the heartache that led them to do this – they are letting it fester and inadvertently saving it up for their own kids to deal with. This avoidance tactic provides a false sense of protection. If we can be brave enough to face the trauma we have inherited head-on, we can save the next generation from suffering the burden.

Caroline Myss explains the difference between curing and healing. Curing is a way of controlling one's past, but healing is an in-depth, active internal process which results in emotional and spiritual recovery. Now I understand how in the past, I had a false sense of control, believing I was healed. In my mind, I had 'cured the problem,' but I had not healed from it. It's no wonder my lessons kept reappearing.

Dr Shefali's work has also helped me understand that healthy boundaries can be used as an excuse to put walls up when one is afraid of doing the inner work. She says we may manipulate ourselves into believing the barriers we create are healthy as an avoidance tactic. I love her 'say it how it is' approach.

From my research, I began to understand that an unhealed soul will never live out her or his potential and is destined to suffer. There will always be an invisible barrier holding us back. We will be frustrated and resentful, and there is no way we can have successful and fulfilled relationships with others if we haven't taken the time to have the most important relationship with ourselves. We may be able to sustain it for a while, but our inner-child wounds will find a way to resurface. It's inevitable.

Lewis Howes, lifestyle entrepreneur, author and podcast host of *The School of Greatness*, explains that our inner child is not healed when it is still hurting, frustrated, resentful, angry or feeling like it has to defend itself from abandonment. He believes trauma causes us to abandon ourselves because we haven't been taught emotional regulation. That is the piece we have to heal inside us.

All my research has helped me to look at my own life and see that whenever I've pushed pain aside, it's become more significant as time passed.

I know now that part of my job is to stop the intergenerational suffering in my family and not to pass it on.

I need it to end.

As my insights grew, I began to make energetic changes which affected everyone around me. I started to send energy, with the intention of healing the core issues in my family as well as Mark's. I sent love and forgiveness without judgement. I hoped for everyone to let go of the heavy baggage they had been carrying around.

Kim and I have many parallels in our lives. We grew up in a controlling environment, had lovely first boyfriends and dated rebellious men (Kim married hers). We are both currently with men who have three children from a previous marriage. The age differences of the kids are almost identical, and they are in the same order of sex: female, female, then male. She and her partner have two biological children – my nieces – whom I adore. Like some sisters who fought when they lived together, Kim and I have grown closer as the years have gone by – more now than ever. Kim has been hugely supportive of me writing this book. After reading one of the early drafts, she told me how proud she was – not only that I had finished what I set out to do, but for digging deep and being committed to so much research. She was surprised at how alike we are after always believing we are extreme opposites.

Kim unexpectedly recognised herself in my story and hadn't realised how much she had put up with in her relationships either. After seeing her life through mine, she was able to make her own connections.

Sharing our stories is a powerful way of impacting another soul. Now I am her support person as she goes through her own mid-life transformation. Previously, she couldn't see her own worth; but recently, she has begun to make positive changes to benefit her health.

The secrets of previous generations hold magic powers to transform and heal subsequent generations. The pain of family trauma remains trapped in our DNA and is experienced as secondary trauma until someone goes hunting to release the demons.

I am grateful to have discovered the treasure map of my own family and to have freed myself – and hopefully others – from future suffering.

29

REFRAMING FIRSTS

We always enter Mark's parents' home through a sliding door on the porch. But one particular Sunday six years into our relationship, we entered through the front door which leads to a tiled corridor. Both walls of which are filled with framed photos – a kind of hall of fame of the family: photos of the kids growing up, wedding photos and family portraits. The last photo is of Mark's wedding to Gina in the early nineties.

I wonder if I'll ever make it up there, I thought.

I remembered once visiting my pop in the nursing home with Mum and Adrian after Nanna had died. We hadn't been there long when Mum's mouth tightened, causing the tendons in her neck to jut out. She got up to fiddle with something on the table. As we were leaving, Mum quickly showed me what she'd hidden – a picture of me with Scott.

'Can you imagine if he'd seen it?' she whispered, gesturing after Adrian.

Mum had helped me dodge a bullet.

After I broke up with Scott, I'd had no previous boyfriends and didn't know the rules or how to behave towards an ex, so we stayed in touch. A few weeks later, I ran into Scott's mum's best friend, Pam, who pulled me aside.

'Hi luv, I know you're probably in a hurry, but I just need to tell you something.' She leaned in close.

'What is it?' I asked.

'If I were you, I'd just stay away from Scott – that's all.'

'Oh. What's happened?'

'Every time you see him or talk to him, he just gets his hopes up. You know – that you are going to get back together.'

'Oh no.'

'Yeah. Mandy said it's painful for him, so maybe it would be best if you cut ties. For his sake.'

I was inexperienced. I didn't know what the protocol was. 'I just thought we could be friends. Keep in touch.'

'I know, darling. But he still loves you. Best to stay away.'

I thanked her.

'No worries, luv. And you didn't hear it from me.'

In my family, exes are kept in the past and are never spoken of. They are history, hidden away in boxes and never mentioned in front of new partners. There seemed to be shame attached to them. Perhaps they represented failure? Best not advertise what didn't work out. A wedding photo from the past would never be displayed on the wall at my mum's home. But it doesn't make sense to me to cut the past out of our lives and pretend it never happened.

So why did the wedding photo of Mark and Gina bother me?

It seemed contradictory that I didn't have a problem with Mark's ex but had a negative emotional response to the photo. Mark and I were solid. Was it more pain, possibly passed down, that didn't belong to me?

I began to explore this a little more deeply. And suddenly, I understood my reaction.

Since I was little, I have always wanted to be first. I *had* to walk out first onto that stage at the end of every year on presentation night throughout high school. I came first in one, two, three and sometimes four subjects out of nearly two hundred students in my year. Success meant coming first. I topped an essay exam in international marketing at uni too. The lecturer handed the papers out from the lowest to the highest mark. I was last to receive mine. First once again.

Coming first made me feel special. I was treated to celebration dinners. Mum and Dad would talk to the grandparents as if I weren't in the room about how I was the smart one. Being first proved it. If I ever received a B on my report card, I'd failed. On the rare occasions that it happened, I cried. *I clearly wasn't good enough.*

To this day, my gratitude journal is weighted towards firsts. The first time we cooked a new dish, the first flower of the season, the first rain in so long, the first time we visited a new country. The media glorifies firsts too. First child, first Mother's Day, first birthday, first home, first kiss, first lover, first job, first time you meet someone, first this, first that.

Firsts are exciting celebrations of a new experience. First means you won. You blazed the trail. First means you get spoilt. Being first was also how Mum received love. As a child, she had been punished by her parents for not being in the top of the class. When she became a parent, she tried to do things differently and would say things like:

'It doesn't matter where you come, just do your best.'

'I was pushed too hard.'

'You study too much.'

'You need to have a life. It doesn't matter if you don't come first.'

But her stories of being grounded and punished for not being good enough weighed more than her words. And perhaps the trauma of this was in the bloodline.

Somewhere, I must have internalized the message: *If I could just come first and make her proud of me, then she wouldn't have to suffer anymore.* I thought I could take Mum's pain away. I didn't know that she had to choose to resolve it. She always seemed resentful towards her parents, and I don't think she ever forgave them. Even though they are no longer here, she has held on to her grievances. She has valid stories of mistreatment and her own reasons for not feeling loved, but maybe her parents were doing the best they could too.

Mum's pain is real. But I also have empathy for her parents. Nanna lost her mum when she was eight so had no role model for how to be a mum. She also had Charcot-Marie-Tooth, a debilitating muscle disease that stopped her from ever driving a car, working or being active.

Pop used to grunt if he wanted something passed to him at

the dinner table.

'Er er,' he'd say as he pointed to what he wanted.

Pop lived in a family where his parents didn't speak to each other (literally) for decades of their marriage and slept in separate rooms. Food was dutifully prepared by his mum and dumped on the table. No-one ever conversed. I also got wind of a family secret to do with his younger sister, but it never came to light. Another one of his sisters died after having a fit in the bath. Who knows what he saw and heard as a child? No wonder Pop was silenced. No wonder he wasn't a great communicator.

As I learned more, I became more compassionate towards my parents. I have never resented them but had often wished they'd understood me better. Now I know that it is almost impossible for a parent to meet all the emotional needs of their children. How could I expect my parents to read my mind and truly know what I was going through? Each parent, having been influenced by the circumstances of their own upbringing, is a human processing their own life. Why are we surprised that our parents are out of touch? Every generation will discover new ways to resent their parents and will naturally regard them as archaic.

I was in the shower one day when it hit me. My entire life scrolled before me into a moment of clarity. I didn't give a damn about Mark's ex. In fact, I genuinely send her love and hopes for her deep and abiding happiness. I have no reason to do otherwise. But I had to come to terms with the fact that I was never going to be Mark's first. The photo on the wall was a reminder of that reality.

We humans are all walking triggers for each other. Our pain is never caused by the person we blame for it. They simply nudge feelings from the past, which are re-evoked and brought to the surface. They don't set out to purposely hurt us. Instead, they inadvertently rip the scabs off sores we have never taken the time to heal.

I'm sure I've triggered past pain for Mark's first wife too. Cathia Leonard Friou's book, *Rock Paper Scissors*, helped me see the other side – Gina's side – the pain of the one who feels replaced and rejected (not because the relationship is over, but what the ending brings up for them from their past). An ex feels ownership of their divorced spouse because they were there first, and have history, memories and sometimes children together. They clutch onto the past to hold on to the power they once had, though it is evaporating while the new partner or spouse is doing all they can to sever the tie so they can have a fresh start.

No wonder 'second time around' relationships struggle. Imagining myself in her situation helped me empathise. I was able to connect with and feel her pain.

The photo on the wall was an opportunity to understand myself better and an invitation to fix the real problem. We can go through life being frustrated and feeling rejected. When I questioned my reactions and kept digging, I found the real reason I felt unworthy: I am not Mark's first. I am *never* going to come first at this. I had no choice but to reframe my long-held beliefs about coming second.

How lucky am I? Firsts are training wheels. Practice. I get the best and the rest of Mark.

When I changed my perspective, I felt liberated.

I finally learnt that my emotions are seldom about the current situation. So much is from my history, from all the generations that precede me. My pain didn't make sense because, again, it was entangled in Mum's.

I was holding on to beliefs that I didn't question. Once I accepted what was real and made my own mind up about how I felt instead of how I was supposed to feel, my angst disappeared, and the universe shifted.

After we were married, we were walking out of Mark's parents' house when he said, 'We'll have to get one of us up there,' as he pointed to the wall.

I organised a framed print of one of our wedding photos that now hangs on the wall below the one of him and Gina.

30

LETTING GO

In the first couple of years in my relationship with Mark, we had countless conversations about babies. He wanted to make one hundred percent sure that I didn't want to be a mother before he had a vasectomy. As he lay on the lounge with frozen peas in his lap, he laughed at me and said, 'I can't give you children now, but I can give you grandchildren. They'll love you as much as me and won't know it any other way.'

But no grandchildren were born yet. And the error of judgement we made in that moment is that they were never his to give.

Some years later, when we were engaged, his first grandchild, Sophia, was born.

Mark was always going to be Poppy, so it seemed obvious

to us that I would be called Nanny. Nanny goes with Poppy, like King goes with Queen. The biological grandmothers had chosen Gran and Grandma. *Nanny* hadn't been used. Mark and I made an assumption that no-one would have a problem with us calling ourselves by these names. And we proudly wrote, 'Love Nanny and Poppy,' on all the cards and gifts we sent in those early years. Perhaps Mark wanted me to be Nanny to his Poppy to live up to his word, his offhand promise – to make up for us not having children.

But when Sophia was three, it was made clear to me – after Mark relayed a terse interaction – that I had no right to this title. I stopped being *Nanny* and was to be called Lisa, and nothing else.

I didn't really care what I was called, but this made me feel excluded and worthless. When Mark and I debriefed my tearful reaction, we realised we had made a mistake – we should never have used this title unless it were offered to us as a gift. I wasn't Sophia's biological grandmother, and I shouldn't have assumed I could use a name that implied I was.

After this incident, I was distressed. I didn't feel like eating, and thoughts kept whirling around in my head. A feeling of dread settled in, like after a fight with a partner – an argument hangover without any argument. Parents have a right to make whatever choices they believe are best for their children in those early years. But I was grieving the loss of a relationship I wasn't allowed to have with Mark's granddaughter.

Back at school, I was the little girl who wanted to be liked, and would bend and contort myself to this end. My entire life, I have wanted to be liked by everyone. But I can't. It's not my job to make people like me.

I had to trust that if Sophia and I were connected at a soul level, we would be brought together again, if not in this life, then in another. It gave me comfort to accept this situation for what it is and not force it to be otherwise.

The Courage to Be Disliked by Ichiro Kishimi and Fumitake Koga helped me to understand that there are 'your tasks' and 'other people's tasks,' and we can get caught up in focusing on things that are not our business.

I finally trusted enough to surrender it to the Universe, God or Whomever Had Control. I became an observer. I sat in my grief and felt it all. I knew from all the work I'd done on myself that there was no other way to get through something other than the hard way.

My writing mentor often quotes Ryan Holiday, author of *The Obstacle Is the Way*. Robert Frost knew it too. He said, 'The best way out is always through.' My old pattern was to ignore what was uncomfortable. I thought it would go away if I pretended not to feel it. Now I gave myself time to process my feelings and not bury the weeds, hoping they wouldn't sprout up again. I also stopped assuming I could understand other peoples' behaviour. I can only change my behaviour and thinking, no-one else's.

Not long after all this, I saw a kinesiologist who helped me clarify my emotions.

'So how do you feel about the situation now?'

'I feel I have actually accepted it. I know I thought I had earlier, but it feels different this time.'

'Mmmm.' She was doing funny things with her hands. Her

fingers were all together in a point as she drew a line in front of my body. Then she looked straight at me and said, 'You really have accepted this.'

'Can you tell I have?'

'I wouldn't say it unless I felt it. Not many people come to this level of acceptance, but I can see you have.'

It was affirming to hear.

'And what have you learned from this?'

'That I don't have to be liked by everyone,' I said with confidence.

'Yes,' she said, nodding slowly.

'It's all meant to be. With the book I'm writing, I am sure to get criticism, so this is great training for me. Not everyone is going to like what I have to say, and I'm okay with that now.'

She nodded again with a smile. The weight I'd been carrying was lighter. It was the first time in eight years that I didn't care about the outcome, or what anyone else thought. I didn't know how some members of Mark's family felt towards me even though I sensed they didn't like me or want me to be a part of their lives.

It was around this time that I began to follow the authors and speakers Rachel and Dave Hollis on social media. I enjoyed the banter of their daily *Morning Show* as I cleaned up after making our juice each morning. The Hollis's generously shared the daily lives of their three sons and daughter Noah (who was two at the time). Little Noah is a sassy soul who radiates beautiful energy. At a time, when I was grieving the loss of my relationship with Sophia, she shone a light for me when

I needed it most. Every day I smiled as I watched videos of her dancing, saying goodnight to her dad and doing everyday toddler stuff. The weekly episode of *Tea Time with Noah* always brightened up my week.

In those moments, I would send love to her on the other side of the world. Being able to witness a small snippet of Noah's life was a gift for me.

I may not be called Nanny, but I will always treat Mark's children as if they are my own blood. Who knows? Maybe it will change our dynamic over time – I've seen other people make it work. I'm envious of the many beautiful examples of non-blood relationships: adopted or step-parents and step-grandparents all around the world who add joy to children's lives. Maybe someday I will get to experience that. But for now, I make do with what I have.

Once we experience the death of a loved one, debilitating health issues or a pandemic, we are forced to accept that we are not in charge. When I relinquished control, I became free to live in the moment as an observer instead of trying to plan an outcome. We are wasting precious time if we are living too much in the past or the future.

I hope circumstances will change to allow me to be part of Sophia's life. But I'm not in control of that – to imagine I am, is to live in delusion. I hold on to hope that as more time passes, old wounds can be healed.

If I can send love to little Noah, a child I've never met on the other side of the world, as well as my nieces, goddaughter and the babies and children of many friends, I can still send it energetically to my step-granddaughter too.

Some things are out of my control. But no-one can decide who I send love to – except me.

31

A PLACE FOR ALL

'We hardly ever talk about other people anymore,' my friend Michelle said recently. 'I mean, gossip.'

It is true. Our interactions of late are about what we've learned as we listen to each other work through challenging situations and explore new ideas. Sure, we talk about her kids, our families and mutual friends, but we rarely bitch or talk negatively. Our conversations are full of encouragement and support.

Anything else is a waste of our time.

Author and podcast host Greg McKeown recently said in an interview that one of his friends admitted to spending 60–70% of his mental energy in his twenties and thirties being angry at other people and about the awful abuse he endured. We all tend to hold on to grudges and dwell on past mistakes, which only burdens us and eats into our productivity. Greg goes as far as saying that forgiveness is a productivity hack because of how much time we waste when we don't forgive.

When I heard Michelle's observation, I took it as a sign that I was finally moving away from my ego and towards my soul. I no longer feel a sense of competitiveness in my interactions with others. After I found the true source of my pain, I've been able to dissolve old resentments, frustration and blame. I regard wise people as vessels of invaluable knowledge, not threats. I choose to surround myself with those I can learn from and who encourage me to expand.

'I spend much more time on myself these days,' Michelle added.

Not only have we stopped talking about others, but we also no longer direct useless energy on circumstances over which we have no influence.

But forgiveness goes two ways. For many years, I'd wasted time regretting my relationship with Todd and was deeply ashamed of myself. I thought that if I revealed my greatest shame, people would no longer love me.

Shame, researchers suggest, is an emotion we are programmed to feel around two years of age, and then we grow up shaming ourselves. Don Miguel Ruiz explains in *The Four Agreements* that animals pay for a mistake once – humans pay a thousand times for one mistake.

After Todd, I felt guilty that I'd ruined Louise's life. But she and I must have crossed paths for a reason. I now understand that we are all perpetrators. We inflict pain on others whether we intend to or not – simply by going about our lives. Just as people come into my life for a reason, I am a contributor in their lives as well. Todd saved me from Scott, and maybe I saved her from Todd. *Who knows?*

I really hope she's found true happiness. I made a mistake many years ago. But we are not the mistakes we make; we are how we choose to respond to them. For many years I hid my secret, afraid I'd be judged. It took me a decade to truly forgive myself for one error in judgement.

Now I feel liberated to finally be vulnerable and able to reveal my deepest shame. It doesn't have any power over me anymore. What remains hidden, remains shameful. Revealing my shame released its hold on me and has helped me heal. It is an arduous process for each of us to own everything we've done. But until we do, we can never reach our full potential. Other people's perception of me in response to my vulnerability is none of my business.

I don't believe any of the hard times in my past were a waste. All I've been through has helped me develop the emotional muscle to manage the pain of being rejected by people in Mark's life when we fell in love. While I was enjoying the best time of my life, I was also suffering the most. I sought guidance from counsellors, spiritual awakeners, kinesiologists and hypnotists to help me. I worked on myself instead of trying to fix or blame anyone else. Some of this confronting work led to many of my breakthroughs.

When I was young, I judged others easily. Now when people act out of character, I'm curious about their pain. What is going on inside to motivate them to inflict suffering on their loved ones and themselves?

When I stopped being afraid to make my own mistakes, I stopped judging others. Brené Brown writes in the introduction of *Daring Greatly*, 'If you are not in the arena also getting your ass kicked, I am not interested in your feedback.'

If we knew that our mistakes and failures would lead to positive outcomes, wouldn't we all live more expansive and fulfilling lives? Imagine if we just jumped into life as if time was limited, without waiting to be ready or prepared. We would all just go for it.

American entrepreneur and author of *Everything Is Figureoutable*, Marie Forleo, says, 'Start before you're ready.' I keep her voice in my head.

The difficult souls we cross paths with have their place in our lives. If they have served their purpose, there may no longer be a place for them. This arrival and departure of people is the natural progression of life caused by changes in geographic locations, death or the simple act of growing apart. We don't have to force relationships to remain as they are. We can set each other free.

Every pairing creates a unique relationship (like a fingerprint) which cannot be replicated. Mark and I click. Our fingerprint works because we are compatible and willing to grow together. We encourage each other to flourish. We also have similar values and beliefs, and want the best for each other. Mark's place in my life didn't fill a void. We came together as whole souls – to help each other achieve our greatest individual potential. We are supportive of each other's growth while being secure and independent within ourselves. We are a great team.

The partners in my past relationships were not a good fit with me to co-create a sustainable fingerprint. Still, I honour them for the time they spent with me and for everything I learned from our time together. I hope they have all found their own happiness.

Why aren't we taught to accept that with every passing minute, we are closer to dying and to utilise the limited time we have to serve others?

What will it take for us to recognise the invaluable contribution we can gift each other?

We all think we are alone in our battles. If only we knew that everyone struggles.

Mark came into my life not just to create the relationship we have together. Meeting him was also the catalyst to my personal growth from the interactions with other members of his family and his wider circle of friends. I am appreciative of all the love and kindness I have received from them. I am especially thankful for the acceptance and love I have received from Steph and Josh who have welcomed me into their lives. Children are our biggest teachers, and because I have none of my own, I've been lucky to receive great lessons from all of Mark's. I've witnessed them transition from their teenage years into their mid-to-late twenties, and I'm excited to see what the future holds for them all.

My parents, partners, friends and family have all had the biggest impact on my growth.

But fleeting interactions can also make massive imprints on our lives. Like the stranger in the café who had a poignant message for me on his biker's jacket. Or the checkout operators at the supermarket, who smile and chat to me when I venture away from the isolation of my writing desk. They aren't to know that I haven't seen another human since Mark left for work and how much I enjoy the banter.

Hundreds of people have played a role in directing my life to where it is today. When Adrian and I were still together, I bumped into our neighbour Ruth at our front door after I'd picked up some pictures I'd had mounted and framed from a diary. They were exquisite graphics with the words: 'Love,' 'Beautiful,' 'Joy,' 'Begin,' 'Sometimes your only available transportation is a leap of faith' and 'You can fly when you want to.'

'What are you doing about all this?' she asked as she twirled her pointer finger in mid-air. She must have guessed or heard I wasn't happy.

In that moment, she nudged me to take my own leap of faith.

'I'm getting there,' I said.

At the time, I felt useless and inadequate. I knew what I had to do but didn't know *how* to do it. I wasn't yet living it. I had laid the path but wasn't strong enough to walk it just then.

I believe we often know what we have to do, but it takes courage to actually live it.

Only in my forties did I begin to appreciate how many of my perceptions of *reality* are just in my head, my *dream*, as Don Miguel Ruiz puts it in *The Four Agreements*. Life is a dream created by our thoughts. None of it is real. Our dream confirms the story we want to portray about our lives and the people in it. We each have our insecurities and tend to use others to confirm our beliefs, which keep us in the past, in victimhood.

In all this, I hope I have helped others on their path too. I may have played a role in causing pain to others, but my soul knows I have been a necessary participant in their development too.

No healing can take place until we change our attitude from 'poor me' to 'thank you.' Instead of complaining about the turmoil people bring, we can reflect on why we're triggered by them. At the core of every problematic situation is something inside of us that needs our attention and our work. I have learned to focus on *what* is unsettling me, instead of focusing on *who* is doing the unsettling.

Elizabeth Gilbert once commented that someone's therapist somewhere knows all about each and every one of us. We are the source of other peoples' suffering, whether we know it or not. When we grasp this, we can practise not taking offence and instead, remain grounded in inner strength and in control of our reactions.

We can only influence what we do from today onwards.

The pictures I framed motivated me like affirmations while I gathered the strength to embody their messages.

Today they hang in my bedroom as a reminder of how far I have come.

I no longer feel I have to protect myself from anyone. There is no-one that can offend me. I have nothing to resent, nothing to fear, nothing left to forgive. Everyone has played their role exactly as they were meant to. The approval and acceptance I have always craved was my own – it had to come from inside me.

32

SEEING CLEARLY

'Yes, master.'

I grew up watching Barbara Eden as Jeannie, pandering to Tony's every whim in each episode of *I Dream of Jeannie*. I observed Sandy being objectified in the movie *Grease*, drastically changing her personality, actions and appearance for the sole purpose of impressing a man. The movie *Sixteen Candles* was a representation of deep disrespect for women. And in one of my favourite fairy tales, *Snow White*, was the one who toiled away all day at home while the male dwarves 'hi-hoed' off to do the important work.

The messages we absorb from our culture and what we are exposed to as we grow up have a profound impact on us. As a result, we subconsciously form unintentional habits of behaviour. I was brought up in an era where there were distinct male and female roles. Maybe that's why I didn't notice what I was putting up with. All my life I've witnessed the mistreatment of women and the way we have been portrayed as the inferior gender in the news, on television and in the media.

When I was growing up, I wasn't exposed to any alternatives other than to accept these gender biases as the way things are. In the cocoon I grew up in, women were subservient in movies, not equal in the workplace and submissive in relationships – always portrayed as the more accommodating and weaker sex. Men had power and ran the country. Women had children and ran the home.

Even though I recognised my mum had some control over the decisions in our household, Dad was the dominant one. He was the punishment enforcer. Mum would announce, 'Wait 'til your father gets home,' and so I knew that the man was the one to fear. It was his job to keep the kids in line.

No person had run a four-minute mile until Roger Bannister did in 1954. Once he broke the record that had stood for the previous nine years, ten others did so in the next two and a half years – the first one just a month later. All Roger did, in effect, was show it was possible.

I believe the fight for gender equality has taken so long because we've not been exposed to enough role models showing us the way. Though once you start researching, there are many women who have bucked the system at great personal cost and sacrifice.

Australian Prime Minister Julia Gillard gave a remarkable speech during question time in Parliament in October 2012.

The speech – now known as the misogyny speech – created headlines worldwide and is still referred to a decade later. I did not blink for the entire fifteen minutes. She had the attention of the world as she professionally defended her position and confronted the opposition leader, Tony Abbott, for his ongoing sexist attitude and derogatory statements against her, and all females, while hardly referring to any notes.

In an interview in 2019, Julia Gillard explained that she was simply mouthing her frustration that had built up over the years. She had bitten her lip over sexist comments for a long time. I resonated with that as I know many women did too.

My whole life, I'd tolerated disrespect from men – looks, words, inuendo and derogatory behaviour. Despite how much distress it caused me, I never spoke up. I never wanted to make trouble, rock the boat or draw attention to myself, so I held my feelings inside and pretended I wasn't outraged or hurt. But the constant silencing takes its toll. The pent-up feelings eventually spill out, as they did when I reached my limit and unleashed my turmoil on Adrian's mum.

'A woman's intensity makes everyone uncomfortable, including herself. We were taught to be nice, not angry, even when our own lives and sanity are at stake,' poet Patricia Lynn Reilly wrote.

Sometimes our reactions come from a place of goddamn relief. Our emotions appear intense because we've been accumulating silences inside. Not only is it tiring – it's unhealthy. We've been trained to supress our feelings because that's what *good* women do. I now realise that I, together with several generations of women, have been brainwashed by the patriarchy. I have been guilty of going along with redundant paradigms. Why else would I have kept quiet and allowed so much silent abuse and coercive control to occur over the years?

Growing up, I wasn't educated on women's rights and equality like the young women of today are.

It wasn't until I reached my mid-forties that I realised I would no longer be silenced at the expense of my own mental and physical health. I was implicitly being an advocate for shutting up and unintentionally validating the outdated patriarchal saying, 'Little girls should be seen and not heard.' Julia Gillard helped me understand how I was perpetuating the problem by not standing up for myself. I had to start setting healthy boundaries in my life. If I had a daughter of my own, I would teach her to stand up for herself and call out bad behaviour, no matter how uncomfortable it felt and how ugly it looked. It's my responsibility to be a role model for others. I have to show up and honour myself, and shatter the patterns that have silenced me.

It's difficult for me to admit that in the past, I was proud of how well behaved I was. I always took the weight of the domestic chores. I slaved away each night for my partners, making meals to satisfy their various appetites even though they sometimes arrived home from work hours earlier than me. Outdated cultural beliefs had me thinking I was a good partner. This is what is referred to today as internalized misogyny, where victims believe the lies that keep them enslaved and disempowered.

I'm sure other women despised the way I made it all appear so easy and perfect. I understand now that people don't connect with that kind of energy. They sense the inauthenticity – no-one has life that organised. These actions leave us competing instead of supporting each other as we struggle – compounding the problems we are attempting to solve. As each day passes, we are learning how strong we can be when we stand as a united force.

As a result of my experiences, I now recognise passive aggressive and narcissistic behaviour from a mile off. I could literally give young women lessons on how to spot a bad relationship with all its warning signs couched in double-speak.

I have yet to meet a woman who hasn't experienced *putting up* with behaviour she never should have allowed, *giving up* her self-worth to gain approval from others and *shutting up* about the things that she should have voiced.

When one of us makes a stand, we give permission for others to follow.

Australian of the Year in 2021, Grace Tame has changed the narrative for young women to speak up about sexual violence. She has helped bring about change to the Tasmanian Evidence Act that made it illegal for survivors of sexual abuse to be identified in the media. The Act was changed in 2020, giving her freedom to raise her voice and reveal her story of being groomed and sexually assaulted by a teacher. She gained attention and encouraged many other women to speak up about their experiences.

All the subtle mistreatment I've endured over the years amassed and chipped away at my soul. I would react very differently now, at forty-seven years of age, but I wish I'd had the courage when I was younger to speak up and say *no* when my partners emotionally abused me, strangers touched me inappropriately on trains and when my ex-boyfriend's father exposed his genitals to me. In that case, the shock was intensified by the betrayal – I had trusted him. Often, the trauma after the event is compounded in the aftermath by the pattern of belief that women are exaggerating or bringing it on themselves. I did not want to go through the distress of being discredited and having to defend myself. This has a name too – secondary traumatization, which refers to the ordeal women suffer at the hands of the legal system when they are called on to rehash the events which have caused them primary suffering.

Until recently, there has not been much support for women who stand up for themselves. Instead, there's been terrible precedence for shushing the mistreatment of women. Looking back, I realise that I didn't tell my dad – or anyone else – about the flashing event because I was fearful of how they would respond. I was anxious Dad might confront my abuser and assault him, and I didn't want Dad to suffer any consequences for what had happened to me. I sacrificed myself to protect another, which inadvertently protected my abuser from punishment too.

But we can only tell our stories when we are ready. I understand why people keep silent and have deep compassion for their multiple layers of suffering as a result.

If I said nothing about all the emotional abuse and manipulation that I have experienced over the years – in relationships, from strangers and known men – how many others are out there who have done the same? I know one thing for sure: the next time a man speaks to me in an abusive or derogatory tone, I will not be restrained.

I was born in Australia in the seventies – a world in which women needed permission from their husbands to leave the country, open a bank account and purchase property. At the time, there were no women in the House of Representatives. In the sixties, there was a marriage bar where women in the public service automatically lost their jobs when they were married. In the seventies, women were still referred to by their husband's first and last name; I would have been called Mrs Mark Benson back then. Sometimes we forget how far we've come.

Why is gender inequality so normalised? The answer is that widespread patriarchal, passive-aggressive, silent social constructs have allowed men to have all the power. We live in a world in which women are still far from equal to their male counterparts. Sexual and gender discrimination remain radical and rampant. Nonetheless, women's rights have started to progress. We now see more women in higher positions and less shame associated with speaking up about mistreatment. Technological changes have helped our cause as evidence can be more easily recorded. I've seen drastic changes to women's rights in my lifetime, but there's still a long way for us to go.

Shows on Netflix and Stan, like *Maid*, *Morning Wars* and *Impeachment: American Crime Story*, are instrumental in spreading awareness of the abuse that has been lurking in our relationships, homes and offices as far back as anyone can remember. *Maid* in particular disturbed me as I watched the abuse of a woman by her partner, feeling as if I'd lived through similar experiences. It's easier to feel the emotions through a character than trying to explain in my own words what has happened to me. What shook me was that every single woman

I've spoken to about it recognised herself in the main character.

What each woman needs to know is that she is not alone, silly, unusual or a failure for being treated badly.

Instead of dwelling and regretting the patterns of gender bias in the past, we must educate each other as we accept new cultural standards of equality.

Women have a voice now more than ever, and each one counts, no matter how quiet or shaky it is. We have to learn to speak up, even if we are nervous and our words don't come out exactly as we intend. Who does anything perfectly the first time anyway? It's more important that we say *no* to being bullied and not perpetuating unacceptable behaviour by tolerating it.

Until men catch up and take women seriously, there will be no real change. But women must speak up about what we will no longer tolerate. We must stop putting up and shutting up.

Let's not forget that there are still many great men out there. Just as we are learning, so are they. I have hope that every subsequent generation will have more respect for each other; and one day soon, every person, no matter their gender or sexuality, will be revered as equals in every sense of the word. We are slowly learning new paradigms. Cultural change in organisations is not instant, nor is it in society. But we can all make changes in our personal lives that impact on the greater whole.

Every transition is difficult. No-one knows what to do. The rules are unclear. People make mistakes and others take offence. Everyone comes from a different standpoint, and we have to learn how to give and take criticism as progress takes place.

In an attempt to move with the times, Mark asked a

group of women in his workplace whether they would prefer to be addressed as girls, ladies, women, everyone or guys, as a collective. Everyone had a different opinion. Some were offended by *ladies*, believing it was an old-fashioned word; and others were offended by *girls*, claiming it was derogatory and infantilising. It's impossible to please everyone in the process of change, but it's imperative that we take steps towards it. Changing a culture that has been in place for centuries isn't easy or instant.

As the cultural environment we exist in evolves, I am evolving; and subsequently, so are my interactions with others. Our relationships cannot help but be a reflection of what is going on in greater society. The partnerships I had when I was younger were unevolved because I was mirroring the cultural climate of the time. Maybe that's why young love often doesn't last. I'm grateful that I met Mark later in life – we might not have been ready for each other if we'd met earlier.

33

CHOOSING MY NAME

Benson is short and simple compared to O'Loughlin.

That damn apostrophe caused me never-ending dramas in every database I've ever been in. That's only one of the reasons I chose to take Mark's surname when we got married in 2018, after seven years together.

There are others, of course.

My humble wedding ended up being an interstate destination ceremony and a week-long celebration with our family and friends. I chose a classic style in the end – with a barn owl delivering our rings. After my unsuccessful relationships with men in the past, I was excited to experience what I hadn't yet, and Mark wanted me to experience the full joy of the wedding of my dreams. Most of all, we wanted to formalise our commitment to each other.

Becoming Lisa Benson signified a definitive fresh start for me. I wanted to let go of the rope I'd held tightly, keeping me safe in my old life. Taking on my new name signified an acceptance of who I am now. I associate O'Loughlin with the little girl with clipped wings who clung to her parents' sides, afraid to be anything but first. Benson is the name I associate with the life that began when I met Mark.

Taking his surname has helped me make a positive shift into another level of consciousness. I wasn't rejecting the old Lisa, but I am emerging as a new version.

I kept my identity, just updated my name.

To some, that may seem like a conventional, old-fashioned choice; but it was my choice, just as I chose not to have kids. Others might choose to keep their birth surname. Some men might take on their wives' surnames. In a world in which more countries now celebrate the rights of anyone no matter their gender or sexual orientation to marry the person they love, we are lucky that life isn't a maths exam where there is only one correct answer. We are each free to do whatever feels right for us.

I grew up believing in fantasies because it was instilled in me. But I am no longer an advocate for fairy tales.

I stopped holding on to the idea – indoctrinated into me, like most young girls – that someone out there would come and save me. Another person never fills a void inside of us. What is missing in us will only be highlighted in the union. When we enter a relationship, each of our inner child wounds are exposed, but we have a chance to heal them in the cradle of that intimacy.

I am in between two generations that hold completely different world views. Each generation is morphing into the next, in the same way the glass beads in a kaleidoscope rearrange themselves to reflect a new pattern. Collectively, we make changes and improvements to the culture that align with new technology, societal values and the altering environment issues. Some people hold on to outdated habits and rituals, and others embrace the new. When I got married, I kept the traditions that served me, let go of others and welcomed new ideas, just as I do with my spiritual practice.

To me, marriage signifies our intention to be together for the rest of our lives.

My story is much more than a love story; it's a self-love story.

This story ends happily – not just because I found my twin flame – that was just an added bonus. I would choose to be single for the rest of my days rather than lose who I am again. With Mark's support, I have found joy from within. We don't need to always agree with each other to accept each other. Co-dependence is unhealthy. I am not defined by needing another person's approval anymore. We have the honesty policy and call each other out when we notice the other falling into old patterns.

I used to feel as if I had to explain or apologise for my relationship.

But not anymore. I don't need to justify finding happiness or feel guilty because others may not have what I have. Everyone is different – I don't compare my life to anyone else's. I spent many years in tumultuous relationships. Now I'm relishing having fun, being loved and seen by someone I love and see in return. I'm not suggesting it's always easy. Every relationship needs ongoing commitment, time invested in each other, and the willingness to make sacrifices. We made a promise very early to keep the lines of communication open. Our honesty policy is sometimes painful, but necessary for our individual growth as well as the longevity of our relationship.

In my story, a wonderful partner appeared when I was close to forty and had almost given up – but not everyone's story looks like this. Yours will be unique to you. I chose marriage and no kids, but you may choose career and no partner, or IVF to parent a child on your own, or any combination of many exciting alternatives. Nowadays, heterosexual women are genuinely weighing whether they are better off on their own and if relationships with men are worth the effort. We have many more choices than our parents and grandparents. That is something to celebrate.

Each of us needs to be satisfied with our own choices. It would be wrong for me to apologize for how fortunate and blessed I feel. It would contaminate my happiness, and I'm done with that. I can't play small or feel guilty. I worked hard to find myself, and by some lucky twist of fate, that led to finding love with someone who treats me well and I want to treat well.

Marriage may not be your dream or aspiration, but I grabbed it with both hands because it's right for me.

Just like some don't understand why I don't have kids, others will never understand why I chose to take my husband's name when we got married. Once again, it's their problem, not mine.

We find ourselves when we honour our own true choices and respect the choices others make.

34

TRUSTING MY FUTURE

'I thought I'd better let you know that I won't be able to go kayaking with you guys in a couple of weeks.'

Mark's daughter, Steph, pulled out a 0000-sized baby jumpsuit from her bag and held it up.

I took a quick breath and burst into tears. Mark and I both jumped up from the lounge to hug Steph and Kyle. They got married the previous year, and this will be their first baby.

After they left, I sent a picture to Steph of the margaritas we'd made to celebrate the news. Steph's reply brought tears to my eyes. She said she wished she could have a margarita and then wrote the words I didn't ever expect to read, 'Congratulations Nanny and Poppy.'

I re-read the text to check I wasn't seeing things. I had

completely let go of the attachment to what I am called, yet here was true acceptance for my place in their family. I have zero expectations anymore and have come to understand that circumstances around us are constantly shifting. Nothing is ever written in stone. And sometimes, when we least expect it, life springs a surprise on us, like this one. I hope in some way, I have an opportunity to contribute and bring joy to this baby's life.

The poet Mary Oliver asks the question, 'What is it you plan to do with your one wild and precious life?' I could give you some grandiose idea of what I want to accomplish – I have many ideas – but the truth is I'm not exactly sure. I am at a place where I don't know which direction I'm heading, but I trust the Universe has a plan for me. Not knowing the next chapters excites me. I have surrendered to being guided wherever I need to be. Maybe my mum's idea for another book, *Where Do I Go from Here?* is where I'll tackle those issues.

I want to keep exploring and learning. I want to delve even deeper and find out more about myself, relationships and life. We put too much pressure on ourselves by projecting way into the future, when sometimes, we can simply enjoy and embrace the moment we are in. The future is merely a presumptuous dream anyway. We expend so much energy anticipating what's next, instead of acknowledging all we have done so far. Writing this book has been a five-year project for me, and I want to celebrate the moment of completion and be proud of myself. I trust that whatever I am here to do will come to me. My purpose will continue to evolve as I share this book, which in turn will guide me to accomplish whatever comes next. I will pick up the breadcrumbs ahead of me as I acknowledge the ones that led me here. Not knowing what's ahead is now invigorating, when in the past, such uncertainty used to frighten me.

For a long time, I've played the role of the rescuer; so it's no surprise that when I started writing this book, I wanted to tell you what to do, what not to do and to save you from heartache. But how could I do this when I'm still learning it all too? I trust that whatever lessons you take from my story are meant for you. It's not for me to get involved.

You will find your own answers in your own way. I can't save you – why would you want me to? I would be doing you a disservice. The hard lessons hold all the magic.

There are no rules and no failures in this life. I have been broken many times. I've put on a great show of appearing in control, but I've made mistakes, gone against my own morals and accidently hurt other people. There have been times where I've been anxious and felt alone. I have made things way harder than they had to be. My own internal struggles were so much worse than anything that was ever *done* to me.

When I was younger, I naively believed that one day in the future, everything would align perfectly. That was before I grew up. Now I am moving forward in my life, honouring myself no matter what it looks like. The road ahead is never fast and direct like a freeway. It's more like a country road, with turns, diversion, potholes and roadwork. Progress doesn't happen in pretty little boxes tied with ribbons. Progress happens in the midst of discomfort – in the shadows of the darkness. Leonard Cohen sings about the crack in everything, which is how the light gets in. The Persian poet Rumi wrote, 'The wound is the place where the light enters you.'

I now have an unfamiliar sense of acceptance, which I have heard is one of the blisses of mid-life. I've stopped forcing. Trying. Fighting. I've dropped my presumptions. Whenever I've acted from a place of *need*, I made the wrong decisions, didn't value myself and attracted the wrong people. Anxiety is the difference between how things are and how we want them to be. I learned true acceptance when I realised I wasn't in control over anything except my thoughts and behaviour. Now there is only what is. Things flow and I deal with them, whether positive or negative. As I let go of controlling the future, I set my ego free.

It's no surprise that from this acceptance, I found the greatest love within. I am whole, without needing anyone else to validate me. I am at a place where I finally see myself. I no longer feel guilty for honouring myself, no matter what anyone else thinks.

We are all flawed humans, and the best we can do is to accept each other wherever we find one another on the path of life.

If no-one else sees my point of view, it doesn't matter anymore. *It doesn't freakin' matter.*

I never imagined this kind of freedom.

Like Julie Andrews in *The Sound of Music*, I want to stand on top of a mountain and sing it at the top of my voice. I own my behaviour, and I don't have to convince anyone I am right.

Who is this – this woman who cares so deeply but, at the same time, doesn't care for other people's opinions anymore?

During the COVID-19 pandemic, I admit I regressed into my old fears. I feared catching the virus and even dying. As I wrote through it, I realised that I didn't actually fear dying. That's going to happen whether I worry about it or not. I feared dying with this book inside me.

I remember Wayne Dyer saying once, 'Don't die with your music still in you.' I didn't realise the intensity of these words until I felt the urgency in my own body. *Why had I not finished my book already?*

It didn't matter that I didn't have a clue what my music was. No amount of trying would have made it appear. The people and experiences meant for me kept turning up when I put my heart into what brings me joy. It's not a coincidence that I met my life partner, writing mentor and many dear friends at a health retreat. That's when I'm in my element. That's where the Universe knew where to find me. I was already playing the music before I even realised it. It was only when faced with uncertainty and the reminder that we are not entitled to a set amount of time that I knew I *had* to finish this book.

I don't have my own offspring to share my legacy with. We pass our knowledge on to our babies, and this book is, in a way, my baby.

Maybe someone out there – perhaps even you – will glean something of value from what I have learned so far. I hope so. This book has felt urgent and important for me to complete and let go. Whether it was just for me – or for you and me – is not up to me. I've done my part. The Universe has placed my story in your hands with divine timing.

I hope I can be an example that no matter how far off track you feel, there are no rules and no time limit to finding your way.

Growing up is a process that happens over the course of our entire lives. The reason I'm so passionate about helping others step into their power and find their voice is that I know the pain of not embracing mine.

My past is my past.

If I am willing to continue to do the work, I will be able to enjoy whatever future I want.

I hope you get to choose that for yourself too.

Conclusion

LET ME FLY

'Think of something you want to let go of. Something you've been holding on to. Say it as an affirmation as you climb,' one of the trainers told us.

We were divided into two groups. *This is going to take hours*, I thought. Luckily, Mark had reminded me to slather on the sunscreen.

We watched the climbers as we waited for our turn. Some only made it to the first rung, some got halfway up, some made it to the top without jumping, and others jumped. You could tell quickly who was going to make it all the way. Some climbed with confidence, others with trepidation. When each person finished, they were given a wet towel for their neck; and we created a human tunnel, cheering and patting them on the back as they ran through. It didn't matter how far up anyone went, we cheered just as loud.

Mark and I were at an intimate Tony Robbins event in Fiji in 2017 called Life and Wealth Mastery. It was a five-day program that focused on mastering your emotions, body, time and finances. On the first morning, we were bussed to the Trapeze. It was our first 'face your fears' challenge, and I was fidgeting while I held onto the back of the vinyl seat in front of me. It was an old-style school bus like you'd see in the movies. We turned on the 'old-style air-conditioning' by opening the windows, and I fanned my face with the tips of my fingers. A salty scent filled the air.

'Are you scared?' Gio swivelled around in her seat.

Gio and Steve were a lovely couple from Florida in the U.S. with whom we'd instantly connected.

'A little bit,' I confessed.

The previous day had been a blur of airports, planes and transfers. I hadn't had time to think much about the Trapeze but had concocted a vision. I visualised a landing, five-metres high, that I'd jump off, catch a swing and fall into a big trampoline-style net. Easy. I even pictured the palm trees and scrub surrounding the huge ledge.

I laughed when we pulled up and saw a scene nothing like I'd imagined. There was an open expanse of grass with two identical Trapeze set-ups. Each one had three poles. Two poles on either side supported the swing-like trapeze. The one in between was to climb. It had u-shaped iron pegs, one metre apart, all the way up both sides. They were thin telegraph poles, for goodness' sake – fifteen metres high. *Where was the expansive ledge I was going to jump off?* How could anyone balance on the incy wincy round bit at the top of a telegraph pole? *Eek*. I wiped away the sweat that began to pool on my chin and forehead.

After jumping, the only support was the safety rope attached to our harness. The slack was released by hand as each jumper descended. I saw a few people hit one of the outside poles as their body spiralled on the way down. I kept telling myself, *Whatever you do, don't hit the pole. Be ready to kick off it. Don't hit the pole, don't hit the pole.*

Mark went before me. He leaped off the top of the pole with all his strength and sprang upwards into the air – arms above his head like a swimmer about to dive into the water. He spread his hands apart with just enough time to grip the swing. He made it look easy. I started to take long breaths as it got close to my turn. Before I knew it, my helmet and gloves were on, and I was all harnessed up. I stepped into the leg straps. There was also a belt around my waist, and straps around my shoulders and neck where the safety rope would be attached. So many times in my life, I'd geared myself up for things but pulled out at the last minute due to my fears – like the Peer Support Camp, or when I made excuses to have the day off instead of competing in the school swimming carnival because I never came in the top three. But in this moment, I was focused. Mark has helped me push through comfort zones, and I was no longer afraid to fail.

My breath went mad. I tried to expel the nervousness out of my lungs.

'Do I go now?' I asked the locals who were in charge of safety.

'Go.' One of the men nodded me toward the pole.

Well, here goes. You're doing this.

'Okay, Lisa's climbing. Let her hear you,' Kris, the trainer, roared to the rest of the group as I stepped onto the first couple of rungs.

'Go, Lis,' Mark screamed.

Cheers. Clapping. People calling my name.

'Go, Lisa,' said Kris.

'Good job, Lisa,' from the crowd.

More clapping. More cheering.

'You've got this, Lis,' Mark's familiar voice boomed again.

'You go, girl.'

Quarter of the way to the top.

The encouragement distracted me from what I was actually doing. What the hell *was* I doing? When my Uncle Brian found out I'd been yacht racing with Mark, he'd shaken his head and said, 'I'm sorry, but I can't actually believe *you* go sailing.'

All my life, my behaviour had been typecast. The good girl who dares not take risks or do anything crazy was about to jump off a freakin' telegraph pole.

'Go, Lisa. You got this.' A woman in the crowd.

'Keep going, Lis. You got this.' Mark had my back.

I didn't look down or think too much, afraid I'd snap back into the person everyone expected me to be. That girl would have freaked out on rung two and stepped back onto the safety of the earth. I heard the supportive voices, but I focused on me. Halfway up, I remembered I was supposed to be repeating an affirmation. It was all happening so fast.

The words that came shocked me.

As a child, I had watched Mum get dressed in front of the rectangular mirror in her walk-in wardrobe. Cross-legged on the floor, looking up at her as she tucked her top into her blue panelled pants (two-inch-wide pieces of fabric sewn together like patchwork, forming long stripes), I thought, *She's beautiful.* Young, trendy, perfect. *I want to be just like her*, I thought.

Now, halfway up the pole, the words came, my affirmation.

'I am *not* my mother. I am *not* my mother. I am *not* my mother.'

Teeth clenched. Squeezing the side of the pole with my thighs as I ascended. I hollered the words in my head, over and over. How many times had I heard my mum say, 'I'm nothing like my mother'?

'You got this, you got it.' An American accent.

'All over it,' Mark called.

'Looking great, Lisa,' Kris bellowed.

I was nearing the top of the pole. There were about five rungs left. *Don't look down. Don't look down.*

Words of encouragement kept coming loud from Mark.

Collective clapping came from what now seemed to be a long way down.

'Take breaths.' Mark again.

I hadn't realised that I *was* holding my breath. Adrenaline had taken over. I was trying to stay alive, repeat, 'I am *not* my mother,' *and* listen to all the cheering at the same time. A calm numbness enveloped my body.

'Come on. Do it, do it.' The crowd.

'Well done, Lis.' Mark.

'Awesome. Wow. Well done.' Kris.

I couldn't actually believe I had reached the top. It sure was a long way. *What the hell do I do now?* It felt impossible to get my legs on top of the pole at that height. But I knew there was only one way down. For one second, my body went rigid, but momentum had taken me too far to turn back.

'Well done.' Mark – a hint of surprise in his tone. 'You got it. You got this. Strong leg up. Strong leg up.'

I couldn't imagine how I was going to balance and lift my foot forty centimetres higher while blowing in the breeze. The top of the pole was the size of a small dinner plate, and it was noticeably swaying. It wasn't flat either; it sloped upwards at the back. I felt like a frog with my hands cuddling the pole and my legs both bent on the highest rungs.

'Hands on top of the pole. Perfect,' Kris encouraged me as I brought one leg up. 'Do the same with your right foot as you did with your left.'

My legs were tired and wobbly.

'When you're ready, Lisa, step up,' Kris yelled in his most assertive voice yet.

He got my attention. I balanced and took three slow breaths, then lifted my body up while at the same time grabbing for the safety rope that was attached to my harness. I was standing on the top of the pole. I was *standing* on top of the pole. My heart was racing but I ignored it. There was so much applause.

'Have a look at the view,' Kris said.

Oh yeah, I thought. It was spectacular. I stood up there and took in the landscape. Banana trees and lush greenery and the water in the distance. The air seemed cooler. Maybe it was the fresh breeze above the trees on my sweaty skin. The expansive horizon drew my attention. I suddenly felt grounded. The ocean, the trees, the birds – I was the only one high enough to see it all. Below me, everyone else seemed so small. I spread my arms out as if I were Rose on the bow of the Titanic. I felt at one with the breeze even though my legs were still shaking. I took a deep, satisfying breath. I was reminded of being back at Mount Conner, once again on top of the world.

Someone yelled out, 'Say something.'

I think I managed, 'Wooooooooooooo.'

I looked up towards the circular steel handle of the trapeze. It was about a foot wide, and the diameter was that of a broom handle. The chains on each side of the swing-looking contraption were tangled around the ropes at the top from the last person. Even a six-foot man would have had trouble diving for it. I was going to grab it though. I wanted to fly up to it and squeeze that bar between my clenched fists. The bar was the only safety net apart from the rope attached to my harness.

'Is this your trapeze?' Kris screamed.

'It's my trapeze!'

'Awesome.'

Then everything stopped. I heard no cheering. I was centred and had no thoughts. I did what I'd never before felt safe enough to do – to *be* in the moment.

And then I jumped.

Without knowing what was going to happen next – or whether I'd land – I sprang towards that bar as if nothing was going to stop me from making it. Not crippled by fear of the unknown or *'What if I don't reach it?'* I, quite literally, took a leap of faith.

I grabbed at thin air. *My* trapeze was too far away. Someone turned the cheering back on. I was on my way down. Spinning and disoriented. There was a blur of colour, then I felt a *whack* on my left shin.

I heard a collective, 'Ow.'

My descent was imperfect and perfect all at the same time. I bashed my left shin into the pole exactly how I'd visualised not doing it. Of course, I did. *You get what you focus on.* Even though I didn't get it one hundred percent right, I did it. I took the risk and I survived.

'Well done,' Mark said when I was safely down, giving me a high ten.

The trainer put a wet towel around my neck, and I ran through the tunnel getting high fives to the sounds of 'Wooo woo wooo woo wooo woo wooo woo woo.'

A lump the size of an egg appeared on my left shin.

'You silly duffer. Are you okay?' Mark said as he gave me a 'we did it' kind of hug.

'I'm all good. I can't believe I did it.'

'You killed it,' he said as we headed towards one of the trainers.

'Rocky, do you have some ice for my leg? I hit it pretty hard.'

'Yeowch,' she said

One of the locals wrapped it in fresh pineapple and ice, and assured me that the pineapple was natural medicine that would make the swelling go down and help stop the bruising.

I smiled as I sat under the shade of a tree watching the next participants do their climb and cheered for them as they had done for me while I clutched my injured leg. I thought about the words that had come to me, the ones I'd never imagined saying. It's not that I didn't want to be *like* Mum. I just didn't want to *be* her.

I wanted to be free to be me.

I don't resent my wonderful mother. I never have. I love her so much that I've sacrificed my own life to live out the one she wished she'd had. I stayed safe so she wouldn't worry. I grew my hair because she wasn't allowed to. I tried to be the perfect daughter for her because she never felt she was that for her parents. She never asked me to. She never wanted me to. But inadvertently, I'd been protecting her and attempting to save her my whole life. I hadn't realised how much of my suffering was tied up in my mother's. It was time to separate from her pain and all the anguish that came before her.

No wonder I had never been free. Until now.

People always said to Mum and Dad, 'Oh, Lisa is so lovely.'

I always took this as a compliment. *Lovely Lisa.* I've been proud of my success at living up to that reputation. But I now see how restraining those compliments have been because they reinforce my performance as a *good girl*. I have been a respectable and responsible daughter. I know Mum is proud of me.

But I need to be authentic, and if that means fewer people will like me, I'll take that over being admired for a false version of myself.

Look out, world, because I am emerging – this is just the beginning of my mid-life transformation. *Legitimate Lisa* doesn't have quite the same ring to it, but I want to live my life authentically from hereon in, even if it means compromising on my loveliness.

Sometimes the path we're on seems to be taking longer than we hoped. But whatever feels hard and challenging is leading to the remarkable. When we've played small so as to fit in, or avoided making people uncomfortable so as not to upstage or intimidate them, we can remember the three-year-old unstoppable child we once were and reclaim her, as I have finally done.

Only in my forties did I begin to ask myself, *Where have I been all my life?*

Now I know that I've been searching for a part of myself while trying to make my mother proud by living my life as she wished she'd lived hers. We sacrificed a lot for each other, trying to protect one another from pain. But in the process, I hid my true spirit from the world. And myself.

Now it is free.

It took my dad dying, for me to realise that I'd been putting up, giving up and shutting up for far too long.

We each learn our lessons when we are meant to. We can't rush them. As we grow up, we do better because we know more.

All that matters is where I go from here and what I choose to do with every precious moment I have left in my life.

I am a woman with a purpose.

I've got a lot more to do, and much more to say; but for now, I am enough.

My dad would have said something like, 'You're mad,' or 'You've got to be bloody kidding,' if I'd told him I was planning on jumping off a telegraph pole.

But I also know he'd secretly have cheered to see his little girl finally free.

ACKNOWLEDGEMENTS

It takes a tribe to write a book, and I appreciate every person who has generously contributed. As each soul touched this manuscript, it deepened and evolved.

Thank you, Alison Arnold, for editing my first draft. Your attention to detail and initial advice helped me work harder to make the manuscript stronger.

There are not enough pages left to thank Joanne Fedler. Joanne, you not only edited subsequent drafts, but you have also been my mentor and friend throughout the entire book-writing process. You have cheered me on from the beginning, you taught me how to write and you also taught me what I had to do to become an author. You have had a significant impact on my life and personal growth, and I am so grateful that you didn't give up on me.

Thanks so much, Norie Enn, for doing the final proofread. I am thankful for your meticulous attention to detail.

Huge appreciation to Lauren Harper from Harper Branding & Design for creating the cover design. I dreamt of a beautiful cover for this book, and your creation is beyond my expectations. You captured the essence of my story and I am proud to hold it in my hands.

Thank you to all of my early readers, especially Xanti and Marcia. Your suggestions were invaluable. Xanti, I am forever grateful for the enormous amount of time you spent on my book, your thoughtful insights and our four-hour feedback conversation. Thank you also to Kerry for reading one of the final versions before publication and the terrific last-minute observations and suggestions.

My Gold and Silver Wings writing buddies – Marcia, Xanti, Kerry, Athina, Mylee, Jan, Brigid, Claire, Cheryne, Marion, Kylie, Louise, Shana, Lorraine, Michele B, Michele H, Judy, Pip, Hilary, Ginny, Dalit, Katrina and Jess – you have helped me more than you will ever know, and I appreciate your support throughout the entire process.

Nailia and her Visibility Challenge tribe – Barbara, Helena and Sonee – you have all been so supportive throughout the process. Thanks for always being reliable and giving honest feedback. Nailia, thank you for believing in me and encouraging me to be seen. Sonee, I feel that we are kindred spirits and have a strong sense that we have lived through another lifetime together.

Thanks to Joanne's Sisterhood of the Rewrite tribe – Anna, Barbara and Sonia – for being the first ones to read some of my words, and your gracious and invaluable feedback.

I cannot possibly name all the wonderful women in Joanne's writing tribe from the Author Awakening Adventure and Write

Your First Draft Masterclass courses. You have supported me more than you will ever realise, and I will never forget the inspirational conversations I've had (and continue to have) with many of you. You have also contributed to my personal growth and spiritual development, and I'm so pleased we crossed paths.

Jane, I've never met you in person, but you are my writing angel, and you always kept me going. You inspired me when I wanted to give up because I knew there would be at least one person in the world who would want to read this book. I am crying as I write this because I see so much strength in you that I don't think you see in yourself.

To my beautiful friends for being my greatest supporters, again too many to name. A special mention to Michelle for sharing countless hours having conversations with me and being a sounding board for some of the themes of this book, Lauren for being my accountability buddy and keeping me on track, Rachael for lending me a computer to start this book before I owned one, and Kristi, Joey and Jo for constantly encouraging me. Thank you to those of you who also read an early draft and gave great advice.

Thank you to Mrs Robinson, who was the best English teacher and year advisor anyone could ask for. You were an inspiration to me in high school, where I discovered my love of words and language.

To my counsellors, massage therapists and spirit guides, especially MaYanya, Sonja, Dave, Karina, Jodie, Sam, Jackie, Mel, as well as the entire Golden Door (now Elysia) team, who helped me tremendously as I processed, wrote and healed, thank you all for your positive energy.

Thank you to my family and ancestors. I am who I am today because of all of you. I hope I have voiced the words that you weren't able to in your time on Earth. I have felt your encouragement all the way, and I know that some of my words are yours, just like some of my pain is yours. I am proud and honoured to be the spokesperson for our family.

To my sister Kim, thank you for being so supportive throughout this journey. I appreciate you not wanting to filter anything I've said even before reading the manuscript and allowing me to have a voice.

Mum, I can't thank you enough for allowing me to share our story to exemplify the effects of cultural conditioning on parenting and how every parent cannot help but have an impact on their children. Because of the themes of this book, I have concentrated on the negative consequences of my upbringing and conditioning, but there was undeniably so much more to be thankful and grateful for. The positive experiences and memories of my childhood far outweigh any negative effects.

I couldn't have asked for a better Mum and Dad. I know you both sacrificed a lot for me, and I love and appreciate you both endlessly. Without you, this book – and I – would not exist.

Dad, I miss you every day, and without the wake-up call of your premature death, my story may have been a very different one. Thank you for being my strength and safety growing up, and for showing me the value of time, and life. I still see you everywhere.

Mark, I can't thank you enough for encouraging me to be my quirky and crazy self. You are my husband, best friend, twin flame and number-one supporter. I couldn't have realised this dream if it weren't for your support. Thank you for being strong enough to hold the space for me as I wrote. You have also reminded me to live for today, and I never take for granted the precious time we have together in this life.

I know it would have been hard and frustrating for you at times as I relived every emotion in my life, but you were always there without judgement. You believed in me even before I believed in myself. Our individual paths aligned, and as usual, we connected serendipitously. You gave me the strength and freedom to fulfil my purpose in this life, which I am eternally grateful for.

I am grateful to the Universe for trusting this story in my hands. I asked you over and over to 'bring this book into my being,' and my wish was granted. Thank you.

ABOUT THE AUTHOR

Lisa Benson is a self-diagnosed recovering perfectionist who spent five years writing her multi-award winning memoir, *Where Have I Been All My Life?* During this time, she lived part time on a boat on Sydney Harbour which she found to be a peaceful and inspirational space for her writing. Lisa and her husband continue to lead a 'double life' travelling between Newcastle and Sydney each week.

Lisa has a Bachelor of Business Degree with a major in tourism and marketing. She previously held various sales and marketing positions in hotels and resorts, and also worked in a real estate office. It wasn't until Lisa was in her forties that she decided to pursue her lifelong dream of becoming an author, and she now writes full-time.

Lisa's motto is *Stop Trying – Start Being* although she spent most of her life doing the exact opposite. Her writing is honest and relatable, and she hopes her vulnerability helps others feel less alone. Lisa would love to inspire women to stop wasting time living up to other people's expectations, to discover the magic of living an authentic life and to be free of self-imposed limitations.

If you would like to hear more from Lisa, you can follow her on Instagram (lisabensonauthor), Facebook (Lisa Benson Author) or LinkedIn (Lisa Benson). Lisa's website is www.lisabensonauthor.com

If you resonate with my story,
I would be grateful if you would take the time to write a review on Amazon and/or Goodreads, outlining how *Where Have I Been All My Life?* has impacted you.
Let's continue to empower women around the globe.

Thanking you in advance, Lisa xx

www.ingramcontent.com/pod-product-compliance
Lightning Source LLC
LaVergne TN
LVHW041623060526
838200LV00040B/1405